PORTFOLIO
THE PROFESSIONAL COMPANION

Subroto Bagchi is chairman and co-founder of MindTree, one of India's most admired software companies. He is India's bestselling author of business books, with titles like *The High Performance Entrepreneur*, *Go Kiss the World* and *The Professional* to his credit. His business book for young adults, *MBA at 16*, was published in 2012.

Subroto Bagchi's books have been translated into Hindi, Marathi, Malayalam, Tamil, Kannada, Korean and Chinese.

Subroto lives in Bangalore with his writer wife, Susmita. They have two daughters, Neha and Niti.

The
Professional
Companion

How to Make
the Best of Your
Workplace Skills

Subroto Bagchi

PORTFOLIO
PENGUIN

PORTFOLIO

Published by the Penguin Group

Penguin Books India Pvt. Ltd, 11 Community Centre, Panchsheel Park, New Delhi 110 017, India

Penguin Group (USA) Inc., 375 Hudson Street, New York, New York 10014, USA

Penguin Group (Canada), 90 Eglinton Avenue East, Suite 700, Toronto, Ontario, M4P 2Y3, Canada (a division of Pearson Penguin Canada Inc.)

Penguin Books Ltd, 80 Strand, London WC2R 0RL, England

Penguin Ireland, 25 St Stephen's Green, Dublin 2, Ireland (a division of Penguin Books Ltd)

Penguin Group (Australia), 707 Collins Street, Melbourne, Victoria 3008, Australia (a division of Pearson Australia Group Pty Ltd)

Penguin Group (NZ), 67 Apollo Drive, Rosedale, Auckland 0632, New Zealand (a division of Pearson New Zealand Ltd)

Penguin Group (South Africa) (Pty) Ltd, 24 Sturdee Avenue, Rosebank, Johannesburg 2196, South Africa

Penguin Books Ltd, Registered Offices: 80 Strand, London WC2R 0RL, England

First published in Portfolio by Penguin Books India 2012

10 9 8 7 6 5 4 3 2 1

ISBN 9780143419198

Typeset in Dante MT by Eleven Arts, Delhi
Printed at Manipal Technologies Ltd, Manipal

ALWAYS LEARNING   **PEARSON**

For Udayan Mitra,
A great professional

CONTENTS

Introduction   ix

Working with *The Professional Companion*   xi

Who Is a Professional?   1

  1. Capacity to Work Unsupervised   5

  2. Certifying the Completion of Work in All Respects   11

  3. Integrity   15

  4. Self-Awareness   37

  5. Authenticity   47

  6. Seeking Help   57

  7. Avoiding False Comparison   65

  8. A Reasonable View of the Future   71

  9. Affective Regard   77

10. Deep Listening   85

11. Reining in Reaction   99

12. Using Your Own Two Hands   107

13. Being Proactive   115

14. Taking Charge: Handling Difficult Situations   121

15. A Personal Vision   127

16. Managing Your Time Right   135

17. Saying No   139

18. The Power of Networking   145

19. Future Vision   155

20. Making an Effective Job Change   163

21. Seeing the Big Picture   175

22. Critical Questioning   189

23. Being Prepared   197

24. Negotiating New World Imperatives   203

25. A Leader among Professionals   215

Professional Resources   223

INTRODUCTION

The Professional: Defining the New Standard of Excellence at Work was my third book and it has appealed to a vast cross-section of readers, from doctors, policemen, teachers, lawyers, software engineers and professional actors to even social workers who have reached out to say how much they could relate to the simple, short and straightforward thoughts on the difference between being professionally qualified and being acknowledged as a 'true professional'. I am no great thinker but I have trained myself to observe well, analyse and appreciate good work—and I curate these examples in my books so that others can benefit from them.

Ever since *The Professional* was released, Udayan Mitra, my publisher at Penguin, has been urging me to design a workbook based on the ideas in it, something that would allow a professional to work by themselves, something that would help them locate where they stand in their professional journey through a broad range of self-assessments. The idea scared me, primarily because I have never designed a workbook in my life. But persistence is one of the hallmarks of professionalism and Udayan has no shortage of it. He kept gently pushing me on how much a practical workbook can help the millions of aspiring professionals across the world to go a step further and put in practice the precepts of the original book. Finally, I agreed—and the result is what you have in your hands.

In this endeavour, I received very valuable feedback from Dr Sumita Raghuram, who teaches at the Pennsylvania State University, Dr Vivek Benegal of the National Institute of Mental Health and Neurosciences, Professor Gautam Rajkhowa of the University of Chester and Ms Lu Ellen Schafer of Global Savvy. I have been greatly encouraged by their attention and kind help. My readers would never know how but they silently present themselves throughout the book and help generously. I am also grateful to my daughter Neha, who has always been a gentle critic of my professional writing. She ran through the early manuscript and gave me her inputs based on her experience as an instructional aid designer drawing from her teaching experience in the Bronx a few years ago.

Finally, I must thank my Administrator, Shanti Uday, who helped with some of the diagrams and the final copy.

Thank you for buying this book; I hope to hear from you, to learn about your experience working with *The Professional Companion* so that we can, together, further improve this book and benefit countless people who not only want to be competent but be admired; people who have affective regard for their chosen line of work.

Please send your thoughts to me at www.mindtree.com/subrotobagchi.

Best wishes,
Subroto Bagchi
Bangalore
1 October 2012

WORKING WITH *THE PROFESSIONAL COMPANION*

'Do I need to read the original book *The Professional* before I go on to this companion workbook?'

If this is a question in your mind, the short answer is: 'No'. *The Professional Companion*, the book in your hands right now, is a standalone book in its own right.

If you have read the original book *The Professional* and then are working your way through this one, it will of course make your knowledge and understanding more refined. But then, many may say, 'I am the hands-on type, I can't read so many books, I would rather try things out right away', and to them, I would just say, go right ahead.

That said, you may, after working through this workbook, actually want to read *The Professional*. While *The Professional Companion* makes you delve into your own self, the previous book has many examples from a varied set of professions and goes on to create a great theoretical base—so reading it will be reinforcement for you of valuable lessons learnt.

This is a simple book. That is because simple is good.

The starting premise for *The Professional* and this workbook is this: If someone is professionally qualified in any discipline, that itself does not make that individual worthy of the term 'professional'. Quite often we think that maybe it is professional competence that makes one a professional. In reality, while professional qualifications and competence are necessary, they are not sufficient conditions for someone to be seen as a professional. For this, an individual must possess, acquire and hone several other qualities.

This workbook will pace you through these qualities. Sometimes it will give you an illustration, and somewhere it will hold up a mirror for you. It will constantly challenge you to look at yourself in a somewhat different manner from what you are probably accustomed to. Finally, the workbook will tell you about additional resources for your professional development.

It will take you a few days to finish this workbook, and you need time for the experience to be meaningful. The best way is to pace yourself. The commitment to professionalism is a lifetime investment, but you can aim to complete the exercises in this workbook in twenty-five sessions. I recommend not trying to squeeze in more than one session in a day. You do need time for reflection, to be able to focus on the takeaways.

This book is designed for quiet, contemplative work. Start with making a physical and mental space that allows you to shut yourself in from the bustle of everyday life: slow down, read a little, think a bit, look at the examples but also look beyond them to reflect on your own rich and sometimes undervalued experiences. Be unhurried. Pause, think and take your time to make sense of things.

Sometimes, I may ask you to write a note to yourself. This is probably going to be the most important part of the inner growth that takes you to the next level in your profession. If there are things you will revisit ten, twenty, or thirty years from now—and thank me for—these are the 'Notes to Myself'.

At other times, I will present an anecdote and ask how you would handle the situation if you were the main character. There are no right or wrong answers here and this workbook is not meant to certify your intelligence or smartness. It is meant to make you reflect, think of possible actions and consequences and help you to build a set of skills that helps you become a better professional than you are now. There are also self-assessments along the way (I do not like to call these tests because many of us will then get caught in the desire to score high). The idea is not to score high but to score right. For every question, try and look within yourself and see who you really are.

None of the above tools will take you to the next higher level of growth; but all of them, used together, will certainly do so.

The book explores a set of twenty-five qualities great professionals invariably have. I have encountered these again and again in my own experience of working with and observing a multitude of professionals at close quarters. This workbook presents these twenty-five aspects in a certain sequence. In the beginning, the ideas discussed are what a young professional must know. In the middle of the book, they are about mid-career issues; and then at the end, you will find critical qualities that distinguish a leader among professionals. Nothing in life is watertight, but I think it will help immensely if you stick to the sequence.

Sometimes I will put you through seemingly inane tasks like pasting your photograph taken a decade ago and, in the box alongside, pasting one that is very recent. Once you have done this, you will see that the two images begin to speak to you in a way you never imagined.

Finally, dear fellow professional, it is fine to use a gel ink or ballpoint pen when working with *The Professional Companion*. However, a pencil is the ideal tool that I recommend. What if you wanted to erase something to write the answer all over again? You don't want to buy another copy of the workbook, right?

Apart from the pen or pencil, I recommend you use a highlighter to mark all the negative answers in the self-assessments. In addition, use the highlighter to indicate your ignorance when the text asks you to answer in 'I know' / 'I don't know' terms. When you have finished the entire workbook, you should go back to take stock of the negative answers and look at all the 'I don't know' responses. The negative answers need particular contemplation and the portions you have shown ignorance of call for further exploration. Together, they are your development plan.

On that note, it is time to get started.

WHO IS A PROFESSIONAL?

Many think that only someone with a professional qualification and training is a professional. That is why we are more likely to think of a doctor, an engineer or an airline pilot as a professional.

In developed nations, the definition is a lot wider. Any person we depend upon for expertise and services, independent of their professional education, is considered a professional there. This could be a physiotherapist, a police official receiving public complaints, a sales person at a retail counter or a service technician at a car dealership.

These are people from whom we expect professional conduct. We seldom ask them about their education and training but we evaluate them through standards of professional behaviour.

It is interesting how the roles sometimes reverse. When these people step out of their professional lives and interact with us, you and I may be their child's teacher, doctor or football coach, and they expect us to demonstrate professional knowledge, skill and attitude.

This means that every profession has a set of sometimes stated but mostly unstated rules of engagement and a true professional embraces these. We expect others to come across as professionals; the same is expected of us.

The origin of the word 'professional' goes back 2000 years to the Latin word *professio* meaning to swear or profess allegiance, akin to a vow someone takes before entering a religious order. A professional has respect and affection for their profession.

Now I want you to pause and think of three great individuals you know, who you have personally come across in the course of your professional interactions, who seem to measure up to the definition of a professional we just discussed—and name them.

1.

2.

3.

Now, take a moment to list the unique qualities you value and admire in them.

—   —

—   —

—   —

—   —

—   —

Use the space below to write a note to yourself on one simple idea from your three role models that you could use the next time but somehow have never really thought about until now.

This workbook follows a format very similar to what you have just accomplished.

In the following pages, one after the other, this book will present you with the twenty-five qualities that I think are essential to be a true professional.

In doing so, we will follow a highly interactive process. Somewhere I may present you with the example of an individual. Then I may ask you to assess yourself against a core quality, not so much to test you but to help you notice the gaps. Only when you have been presented an idea, an example and a simple self-assessment will you be able to do some sense-making at your own pace. It is then that lasting improvement can come through an action plan for the future.

1

Capacity to Work Unsupervised

Many people have difficulty producing their very best without being watched over. When you know someone is watching, you come and go on time. These days, it is commonplace for employers to allow an employee to work from home. Now, if I'm working from home, no one knows if I am doing my work or doing other things. Even at work, people surf private sites, send e-mails to family and friends or are on the phone sorting out private issues slipping into a meeting room or lingering in the cafeteria. When the boss sets the deadline, you meet it. When the customer demands it, you go the extra mile. No one is the wiser about what you do with the rest of your time.

In today's world, any form of supervision is an overhead and the workplace necessitates that we be responsible for not only our work product but for doing our work diligently without any need for supervision.

An amateur needs supervision; a professional can work unsupervised.

Think of a situation like this:

Aniket is a young law graduate. He is asked to draft a new agreement. He does not find the assignment interesting. He cuts and pastes clauses from previous agreements with other clients and in doing so, while the broad requirements are met, he forgets to scan the document for the earlier names and specific terms. The document goes out with other people's names in it; worse, the contract amounts mentioned give away a lesser price that was quoted in an earlier instance. The management sees red when the prospective client calls up infuriated.

In the space below, recount any similar situation where a half-cooked document has gone out because the draft was not read by someone internally and has caused pain to the organization.

Now, answer the following questions for yourself. Please be honest to yourself. Remember that no one is watching!

	Yes	No
1. I know who the customer of my work product is.	☐	☐
2. I also know my customer's customer and how my work impacts them.	☐	☐
3. I set up my own work targets every day.	☐	☐
4. I look at my own work and monitor myself against how well I am doing.	☐	☐
5. I don't give excuses.	☐	☐
6. I always do my very best each time I take up something.	☐	☐
7. I do my very best every time if there is pressure of being watched over.	☐	☐
8. I do my very best when I am in a good mood.	☐	☐
9. Sometimes I goof off if my boss is away for a few days.	☐	☐
10. Sometimes I goof off after telling my boss.	☐	☐
11. If a client is not very demanding, I can take it easy.	☐	☐
12. I may reach my work late without informing my boss because I know he/she has an outside meeting.	☐	☐
13. Since I finished my given project ahead of time and my supervisor presumes I may still be busy, I do not report completion and ask if I could be of any help elsewhere.	☐	☐
14. I ask for additional work whenever I have a freed up space.	☐	☐
15. I am as productive at home as I am in office, whenever I am working from home.	☐	☐
16. I can visit the beauty parlour during work hours as long as I get the work done on time.	☐	☐
17. I seek feedback from my customer.	☐	☐
18. I seek help proactively.	☐	☐
19. Customers and co-workers seek me out.	☐	☐
20. I do not feel overwhelmed with my work.	☐	☐

Now, look again at your responses and see what they might be telling you about your ability to work unsupervised.

It is amazing how many of us actually do not know who the recipient of our work product is. This is more pronounced among professionals who work for large organizations. Unless we can humanize who our customer is, it is difficult to bring out the very best in us. Working unsupervised is not about simply meeting expectations, but excelling regardless.

2

Certifying the Completion of Work in All Respects

Increasingly, we live in a world in which only we may know that a given work product is complete in all respects.

The nurse who stitches up a patient after the surgeon has operated could do it in many different ways. Only she knows that the job has been done perfectly. A physiotherapist alone knows if the required intervention is over and the session has delivered its full worth. A teacher creating a lesson plan is the only person who would know if it was done in the best way possible. A news reporter is the only person who can tell if there wasn't another interviewee who could have been reached out to to give an opinion and whether a story has been fully researched and that all source checks have been done. A copy writer in an advertising agency alone knows if the work output could have been done better, but for the weekend binge. Only a software designer or an architect knows whether or not a code or a blue print could have been done any better.

The story goes that a sculptor was spending an equal amount of time beautifying the back of a piece of sculpture as he had spent on every line and curve in the front. Someone asked the sculptor why he was spending so much time on the back which no one would ever see. To that, the man replied, 'God will see.'

How often have you come across a tailor who has delivered a custom suit but forgotten to remove a few threads here and there?

Have you ever received a nice gift that has been poorly packaged in a previously used box and crumpled wrapping paper?

Did you ever notice the grease marks on your dashboard after the car came back from servicing?

Have you ever come across a situation when your doctor prescribed an antibiotic but never told you to watch out for the side effects?

Only a painter knows when all the brush strokes are done and the painting is really complete. The same is true of every individual's work these days.

We must ask ourselves whether we understand the meaning of completion and pause to look for signs of it each time we do something.

Write in the space below about one instance where, as a customer, you were satisfied about a piece of work delivered—but just as you were about to leave, the service provider asked you to hold on and then did something extra that exceeded your expectations.

3

Integrity

Dictionary.com, a very useful, free website on the Internet gives us the following meanings of the word **integrity**:

- adherence to moral and ethical principles; soundness of moral character; honesty
- the state of being whole, entire, or undiminished: *to preserve the integrity of the empire*
- a sound, unimpaired, or perfect condition: *the integrity of a ship's hull*

What are words similar to or synonyms of integrity? They are rectitude, probity, virtue and honour.

Sometimes, what may be similar to something does not quite explain its character. The same website that has so many words to explain what integrity may be has just one word to describe what it isn't and that word is **dishonesty**.

> Professionally qualified people who are not honest cannot ever be considered professionals.
> Integrity is a quality that demarcates or separates skilled or even competent personnel from a true professional.

Think of a doctor who steals human organs from unsuspecting patients and sells them. Is he not competent at his work? Of course he is—that is how he accomplishes his work. But is he honest? No. Would you and I ever like to be treated by such a man?

Or think of a highly qualified lawyer or a doctor who receives confidential information about you and shares it with another person. Worse, trades it for money. Would you like to have a professional association with such a person?

The following are examples of people with great qualification and competence who lacked integrity. That one failing kept them away from the Hall of Fame of professionals despite a lifetime of work—and in reality brought them disrepute just as they were about to reach professional immortality.

- Rajat Gupta, the first Indian to head McKinsey, was found guilty of insider trading. Immediately after a board meeting at Goldman Sachs, where he was a director, he phoned his stock trader friend to tip him off on the board's decisions. The latter acted on the tip and immediately purchased Goldman Sachs stock.
- Calcutta High Court judge Soumitra Sen resigned in ignominy after the Rajya Sabha voted to impeach him on charges of corruption. The judge had misappropriated public money.

How can you and I practise integrity in the course of our work with others? It is not a complex thing at all. We need to keep four simple things in mind:

1. We should follow the law if a law exists

2. We should use fair judgement if there is no law

3. We should seek help if we are in doubt about something we are about to do; we should question whether it would breach integrity

4. We should ask ourselves before doing something whether our act, if discussed publicly, would cause us shame or embarrassment

Whoever follows these four principles will act authentically and live a life of integrity.

Think about the difficulties in following these four principles.

Now, write about someone you know who may have done well, or for that matter not done well, by following these four principles. Who are these positive or negative examples?

People I admire for their integrity:

People who I think lack integrity:

It is never easy to follow the right path. History is full of examples of people who have paid a personal price for being honest, for displaying integrity. Whether or not you will follow a path of integrity is always a matter of personal choice.

The book *The Professional* tells the fascinating story of Mahadeva, a gravedigger in Bangalore.

Mahadeva has dedicated his life to burying unclaimed dead bodies. His job is difficult. It requires no great skills learnt at college; yet he exhibits the true qualities of a professional more than many white-collar workers out there.

Mahadeva came to the city with his poverty-stricken mother. Sometime later, she fell sick and was admitted to the government-run Victoria Hospital, where she passed away. Mahadeva grew up in the precincts of the hospital and started running errands for patients there to make a living. One day, the police asked him to bury an unclaimed body (bodies that are unclaimed are disposed of after three days).

Mahadeva had found his vocation—he became a specialist at burying unclaimed dead bodies, on a turnkey basis. He did his work with such dedication, focus and care that soon he was much in demand at every hospital in Bangalore.

He bought his own horse-drawn carriage for the job. After the horse died, people who had come to know him pooled money and bought him an auto-rickshaw. A picture of the horse is Mahadeva's logo today. His son has joined him in the business.

Mahadeva has buried more than 42,000 corpses in his lifetime; the chief minister of Karnataka thanked him for his selfless service to the abandoned citizens of Bangalore.

Mahadeva is the perfect example of a high performer and a true professional because once he is handed over a body for burial he does not need supervision. He can certify the completion of his work and demonstrates the highest standards of personal integrity.

As an orphan on the streets of Bangalore, Mahadeva could have chosen a life of crime; it was probably the most convenient option for him at that time. But he chose a life of hard work and dedication. He chose the right over the convenient.

In the space below, write down a very personal anecdote from your own life that shows someone you know who acted with integrity, and chose to follow the right path and not the convenient.

Now let us look at a few situations taken from real life. What would you do if you found yourself in these situations?

You have recently joined a company and it is imperative that you prove your worth. There is a competitive bid you have submitted to win a major deal and its favourable outcome can put you on the fast track. Your friend who works for another company says his brother-in-law is the procurement officer with your prospect company and he can give you the inside story. He does not really need a bribe but later on if you can arrange an overseas trip for him and his wife for a week to Thailand (you do not have an office there) he could even get you the deal. What would you do?

- Tell your friend to choose a tour package but be reasonable
- Ask for a direct deal with the brother-in-law
- Thank him for the offer, laugh loudly and tell him he must be joking

Your company pays for the healthcare of your family through an insurance scheme. You have never claimed any reimbursement till date. Last night your spouse had a blackout and you rushed her to the nearby hospital. They kept her under observation, did all the tests and found nothing. Thank God, she is feeling better now and everyone thinks it may just have been fatigue and low blood pressure. The doctor says you can take her home. The hospital charges are Rs 16,000 and insurance would not kick in unless she is kept in the hospital for twenty-four hours. It has just been eighteen hours.

Will you ask the doctor to keep her for a few more hours even though she is fine and could go home? The choice is between paying the money yourself or getting the insurance company to pay. No one in the office would know either way. What would you do?

- Get her discharged and pay up the amount
- Request the doctor to keep her overnight by stating on paper that she may be at risk if discharged
- Call your friend who always stands by you and fully supports your views on everything

Your child desperately wants a job in a software services company. Such companies do not visit his college as it is not on a par with where they go to hire fresh graduates. He says that there is another way to get a software job and that is with work experience. Your son says that his friends have procured a genuine-looking experience certificate for Rs 25,000. He could repay you that money in three months if you let him do what his friends have done. He says some seniors at college have done the same and got jobs. You love your son very much and want his dreams to come true. Which of the following would you do?

- Tell your son that you do not have the money
- Tell him that if this is the only way to get a software job, you can borrow the amount but he must repay it
- Tell him to seek an alternate career that does not require such a certificate

You are the service technician at a leading automotive dealership. People respect your workmanship. A rich client drives in with his expensive car and says the motor controlling the rear left door glass is not working. He says, 'Do whatever it takes' and goes away. You open the part and find that it may work for a year and a half more for sure.

There is a 'sell more parts week' on at the dealership and you are an inch away from winning two tickets to Malaysia. You and your spouse have never been abroad. What would you do?

- Replace the part and send the invoice to the owner
- Call the man and say you could replace it if he wanted but you believe it could work for another eighteen months if repaired
- Ask your manager to suggest what would be good for the dealership

You have applied for a job as an assistant editor at a newspaper company. In the final round of interviews, they say you can have the job and it entails a 50 per cent raise over what you get now. They have not, at any stage, asked you if you are married. You are and your spouse works for a rival newspaper. What would you do?

- Follow the don't-ask-don't-tell policy
- Ask them about company policy in general and see if it asks for disclosure
- Let them know about your spouse up front and risk losing the job

Your company prohibits the use of company resources for personal use. Your cousin wants to borrow your laptop for the weekend. She lives a block away and is quite reliable. What would you do?

- Show her the company policy
- Let her have the laptop because the weekend is your time anyway and saying no to her would make you look like a prude
- Gently tell her it is an awkward thing to do, and neither she nor you should do what is not appropriate. In the process, you do risk losing her love for you

You undertook a week-long overseas trip on official work. At the end of it, you find that a receipt for a food bill is lost. What would you do?

- Add an additional zero to the taxi bill
- Wait for the next trip so that you may show a personal spend as official
- Ask your supervisor what to do

You are the private wealth manager of a leading bank. On Friday you are told that an audit team is coming over on Monday. They will audit all documentation. You find two pages of a client undertaking in a dossier does not have the client's signature. These are not pages with financial information and just contain standard verbiage. The client is not in town. Your friend suggests you mimic your client's signature—just initial the pages. It is a much done thing. No one may ever know. Would you:

- Sign
- Ask a friend to do it and return the favour sometime
- Call your father who is a retired man and ask for his opinion

You are seeking fire department clearance for your next office building. The contractor has come back and asks you if he can pay a bribe on your behalf instead of running around for three weeks. He says he can raise a bill for digging a tunnel that would not be, in reality, ever dug. Which choice would you make?

- Meet the fire services officer you have never met knowing full well that he will make you come three more times
- Ask your chief executive to accompany you to the meeting
- Ask the contractor to pay because that is the only way things work

THE INTEGRITY TEST

Given below are a set of situations in which real people had to make decisions that defined their standards of integrity. Give yourself a chance to consider what you would have done if you were in their shoes.

1. Your company allows medical reimbursement against your flexible pay package that entitles you to a tax shelter. Your friends submit fake medical bills but they actually buy cosmetics and other items of daily need from the pharmacist instead. They say the money is in any case their entitlement, so how does it matter to the employer what they are buying? In any case, it's a prevalent practice. Would you do the same?

2. Your company allows you to travel first class by train. Your colleagues who are travelling with you decide to go second class but charge the first class fare and keep the balance.

3. Your customer asks you to over-invoice the purchase of a machine to the company so he can keep the differential amount for his personal use.

4. Your customer shows you a competitor's proposal and says you can take a photocopy of it and make a winning bid. The customer is very happy with your past relationship and is encouraging you with inside information.

5. You have gone to recruit from an engineering college on behalf of your company. The college gives you a gold ring as a gift. It seems to be an industry practice.

6. You are arguing a case for the state; the defence lawyer asks you to modify charges and take a part of his fees paid by his client.

7. Your friend wants you to lend him your company car—which is for your official and personal use—for the weekend.

8. You are the HR head of your company. Your brother-in-law has been selected as a management trainee on his own merit. Your friend in the recruiting team says it is nothing to be concerned about.

9. Your editor asks you to interview the CEO of a company. After the interview, the CEO offers you an expensive Mont Blanc pen with your name engraved on it.

10. You have referred your patient to a polyclinic for tests and they have sent you a thank you card with Rs 5000 as a referral fee.

11. You have bid for a project. The customer wants you to inflate the price and offer him a ticket to Switzerland for his wife who would accompany him for a training that your company will pay for. That training is standard practice for the purchaser and you would normally pick up that portion of the expense.

12. You have knowledge of the company's quarter results that are not public yet. Your niece wants to know if it is a good time to buy company shares from the open market. She will be upset if you do not tell her.

13. You know it is against company policy to misuse company resources. Your boss is regularly downloading and watching pornography on his company laptop.

14. Your boss has taken his wife on a trip to a holiday destination and is asking you to sign the bill as a customer call.

15. Your married colleague is regularly asking you to come home when her husband is on tour and asking you to stay over.

16. Your boss is asking you to sign a financial report that you have not read at all. He says, 'Don't worry, trust me.'

17. You find your subordinate has submitted a fake qualification certificate but he is critically needed for a customer project that is extremely valuable.

18. Your most important supplier offers you a golden retriever puppy because you love dogs.

19. Your company allows sick leave. You want to take time off to prepare for an important examination and a local doctor will give you a certificate to state that you were hospitalized with a broken leg.

20. Your interviewer is asking you if you can bring along a file of your current employer.

21. You have a critical software deliverable; there is free code available from the Internet for non-commercial use.

22. Your software project requires extensive use of a tool for six months. An evaluation copy is available free for thirty days but you can download it under different user names every month for six consecutive months. No one will know.

23. Your supplier is offering you six tickets to a musical performance followed by a gala dinner.

24. Your senior is asking you to sleep with him in exchange for a promotion you badly want.

25. You would like to buy a car from the same dealer who supplies vehicles to your organization.

26. Your wife wants the company architect to design your house. He is really good.

27. Your friend gives you her card and requests you to swipe it for her the next day. She needs to see her doctor in the morning; the boss is a nasty guy who does not give people leave easily but he is on leave himself tomorrow.

28. Your company allows you to lease a car. Your brother-in-law's vehicle is lying idle and he suggests you show it as a leased car.

29. Your boss is throwing a party at home for his friends and wants you to expense the crate of alcohol as business expenses.

30. Your friend wants you to sign a fake employment certificate. He has left the company and no one will know.

31. The auditors are here for a crucial certification. They want you to self-certify certain implementation but you yourself have not really verified the facts.

32. Your devoted secretary wants you to allow her to avail of the work from home policy to appear for an examination.

33. A patient under your care was given a wrong injection by mistake. Your subordinate has done it and says she will never do it again. She requests that the patient not be informed.

34. Your boss wants you to arrange for paid internship for his son at a supplier's site.

35. The local police station in charge wants to come every day after work and have complimentary drinks at your restaurant. He can cancel your bar licence if you do not oblige.

4

Self-Awareness

'Who am I?' is not always as deeply philosophical a question as we may think. At one level, of course, it may be something that great spiritual masters struggle with and are unable to answer. But just look around you and think of professionals you admire: your hairdresser, your child's paediatrician, a teacher you have always respected and admired. Then think of one simple quality that is common to them all.

It is likely to be that you feel they are authentic individuals.

They come across as real. They do not seem phoney. That is why you feel comfortable with them. That is the reason you are okay discussing your problems and issues with them, seeking their expertise and literally handing over your affairs to them. They know who they are. They are not puffed up.

In the world of nature, animals usually puff up when they apprehend danger. Puffing up is about pretending that you are someone who in the normal course of life you are not. Because people who puff up perceive some threat deep down, they assume a proportion that is not really them. As soon as the danger goes away, the puffed-up animal—a frog, a snake, a fish or a porcupine—quickly returns to its normal state. The puffed-up state is abnormal and actually stressful.

Many people walk around in a perpetually puffed-up state. It shows on the outside and creates stress on the inside.

If you go back to the question about your favourite professionals, you will realize that they never come across in a puffed-up state. They are comfortable in their own skins. How are they able to be themselves? Are they born self-aware? Can you and I be self-aware? Can self-awareness improve as we go along?

Here are a few simple things you and I can start with.

It begins with a simple question: Who am I?

Please take a few minutes to write down the answers to the following questions:

1. Who was I born to? Write a few sentences on your parents and describe their circumstances as young people as you have heard the story from them.

2. Write from your early memories about where and how you grew up.

3. Take a few moments to think of and reflect upon the turning points in your life and who influenced them.

4. Think of three people from your early childhood and young adult days who were as good as you were and could have been where you are today, but somehow never made it; people who for some reason you have left behind.

5. Could you have been them? If not, why not?

6. How often do you, in the normal course of your day, remember where you come from?
   - Often
   - Only rarely
   - Almost never

7. How much of your current success do you attribute to factors beyond you?
   - Very little
   - Some
   - A lot

8. Who was principally responsible for the setbacks in your life?
   - I
   - Other people who didn't like me
   - Circumstances

9. How did you recover from the setbacks in your life?
   - People helped me
   - Fate helped me
   - I took charge of my life

10. You took a hard position on a particular issue at work the other day. You won the cause. A few days later, you found mistaken assumptions in your earlier position. Are you more likely to:
    - Move on
    - Immediately call for everyone's attention and apologize
    - Focus on damage control

The idea of the self is always relative. If others do not exist, nor do I.

The self-aware professional invariably—and often—acknowledges the beneficial role of others in their life. When in a difficult situation, they take charge of their own recovery and do the best they can. They put other people ahead of themselves and do not feel awkward if a mistake needs to be publicly acknowledged.

Self-awareness begins with being constantly aware of and proud of our beginnings and then by being grateful for how far we may have come.

It is most powerfully captured in the speech Steve Jobs, the founder of Apple, delivered at the commencement at Stanford University in 2005. As part of his speech, Jobs pointed out how in retrospect our lives are all about 'connecting the dots'. He recounted how he was given away for adoption by his unwed mother, how he dropped out of college and the story of his life as it unfolded.

If you are not familiar with this inspirational speech, please do read the full text and watch it too at http://news.stanford.edu/news/2005/june15/jobs-061505.html.

Ask billionaire Narayana Murthy, co-founder of Infosys, and he will proudly tell you about his father who was a schoolteacher in Mysore. When Murthy was selected for admission at the Indian Institute of Technology, his father could not afford to send him there and asked him to study in the local engineering college instead.

Narayana Murthy is also proud of the fact that when he started Infosys the seed money came from his wife, Sudha, who gave him Rs 10,000 to start the enterprise.

Not to be ever compared with these great people, I always remember my own ordinary beginnings. I was born to a lower-middle-class family, and grew up in government housing with no electricity and water. I started as a lower division clerk in a government office and turned up for my first corporate interview in borrowed clothes.

I remember my benefactors, however small their contributions may look like from my current position in life.

They are important to who I am today.

5

Authenticity

The authors James Gilmore and Joseph Pine II, in their book *Authenticity*, sum up the importance of authenticity very nicely in these words: 'In business today, executives recognize that their leadership skills hinge largely on their ability to gain a reputation among employees as real.'

In a globally connected world in which we are besieged with an abundance of goods and services, people are constantly seeking out the authentic. Authenticity is always at a premium. All things remaining the same, we all want to deal with buyers, suppliers, co-workers and other professionals who are authentic. Customers, increasingly aware and informed, want to favour companies that they believe have authenticity beyond just quality goods and services at competitive prices.

But what is authenticity?

Why do some people come across as authentic and others not?

Am I authentic? Am I authentic to some and not to others? Can I practise authenticity?

Being authentic is being original, being you.

It is about honest intentions, transparent acts and acknowledging your own limitations, what you can or cannot provide even at the cost of sometimes losing out on an opportunity.

Authentic people do not have dual standards. With them, 'what you see is what you get'.

The best way to think of authenticity is to ask why a certain neighbourhood grocer, vegetable seller, fishmonger or butcher has more of your trust than others in their trade. Or a bike mechanic who would rather lose a customer than compromise on his reputation. When he says this oil filter needs a change, you absolutely do not question the man. Similarly, why a certain paediatrician seems to be *genuinely* listening whenever you talk about your child's health problems while another appears to be superficially engaged.

Authenticity, contrary to what many of us think, is nothing esoteric. It is about small professional attributes, transparency and predictability.

Being authentic is not about being the best. It is about being who you are.

When I was a small boy, a friend of my elder brother's visited our house. The school results were just out and, as was customary in Indian households, my father inquired how the young man had fared in his examinations. 'Well, I *almost* got a first class,' he replied.

My father was taken aback. In his world, either you got a first class or you didn't. What was an 'almost first class'? The young man explained somewhat diffidently that he had scored 58 per cent marks. That, technically and in reality, was a second class, not a first.

From that day on, in our family, whenever someone was pushing the limits in any matter, the repartee was, 'Almost first class?' The point is that one needs to be truthful and confident about one's achievement; it doesn't matter if it falls short of a certain benchmark.

Here's another story. I once took a customer to meet Azim Premji, chairman of Wipro. The customer was in complete awe of Premji. So, instead of Premji courting him, from the very moment he took his seat, the customer went on and on about what a great company Premji had built and what a grand vision he had created et cetera.

After listening politely for five minutes, Premji said in a dignified voice: 'Thank you for your kindness but please do keep higher expectations from us.' He wasn't going to get carried away that easily.

Many years later, I was at the Bangalore airport. I had checked in for a Jet Airways flight. Just then the Kingfisher station director saw me and invited me to use her lounge. I protested mildly but wasn't going to press beyond a point that I wasn't flying her airline today, and though it was nice of her to make the offer, it didn't really look nice for me to accept. She however persisted and asked me to meet her after security and then went ahead of me to the other side.

After a few minutes, just when I was coming through security, I saw her speaking to Narayana Murthy near the airport bookstore. He seemed to be making an emphatic point to her. I walked up, said hello to Murthy and asked what the matter was. He said, very seriously, 'She is doing her dharma and I am doing mine.'

It turned out that Murthy too was flying Jet and she was asking him to use the Kingfisher lounge but, unlike me, Murthy was completely firm that it was not in order.

Greatness comes from practising authenticity in small things.

Answer the following questions for yourself:

	Yes	No
1. In a personality test, are you likely to give answers that show you in the best light?	☐	☐
2. When people call for you, do you sometimes tell your colleague to convey that you are not in?	☐	☐
3. You need a specific favour from someone and call him on the phone. You are more likely to:		
a. Precede the conversation with small talk	☐	☐
b. Just say what you need	☐	☐
c. Tell him up front that you do have a specific reason for calling today but that you would also want to know how things have been with the other person because it has been a long time since you have been in touch	☐	☐
4. When sending out customer feedback surveys, you are more likely to send a mailer to:		
a. Those who will give positive feedback	☐	☐
b. Mix up the customer list and draw lots and then send the survey to a small group	☐	☐
c. Make sure all unhappy customers get the survey	☐	☐

	Yes	No

5. You have a new boss who is warmly complementing your team for an excellent job done for a great project delivered to the client. The client side wants to give out a large financial reward. There is one small issue. The lady who had initiated the work from the client side no longer works with them. It was she who actually created the design and your team implemented it. On your side, there was an engineer who had done more work than the others in the early phase and he has since left the company. How likely are you to do any of the following?

   a. Write to your boss and the client that while the reward is a great honour, it would just not have happened without the lady on their side and your man who has left you   ☐   ☐

   b. You would not probably do (a) above but are very likely to acknowledge them at the award ceremony   ☐   ☐

   c. You would be the first to suggest to your boss and the client that the reward should be shared with the people who have left because of their significant contribution   ☐   ☐

6. You have a new subordinate who was earlier working for someone else. She is not regular at her work. She has been parked in your team for three months after which she will be on maternity leave. Which is the most likely option you would exercise?

   a. Let her be   ☐   ☐

   b. Call her and tell her that her approach to work is not acceptable   ☐   ☐

   c. Ask your secretary to tell her to be a little more careful   ☐   ☐

	Yes	No

7. A prospect is praising your capabilities to the high heavens. You do not think it is well deserved. There could be a few risks as the project begins but you have reasonable confidence that they would be addressed. Given the quagmire, which of the following would you do?
   a. Take her aside and caution her to set the right expectations ☐ ☐
   b. Bask in the moment ☐ ☐
   c. Tell your boss about it ☐ ☐

8. A key member of your team wants to quit. There is less than a 50 per cent chance that he will stay back even as the company is making efforts to retain him. It is on his strength that you have got a large contract and the client has often told you so. Which of the following you would do?
   a. Stay put because you don't know the final outcome— what is the point of unsettling the client? ☐ ☐
   b. Send an e-mail to the client informing him ☐ ☐
   c. Call the client and break the news in person and seek help in retaining the colleague ☐ ☐

9. You did your MBA at Acharya Institute of Management (AIM). When you meet strangers and do small talk, do you usually say you did your MBA at:
   a. Acharya Institute of Management ☐ ☐
   b. AIM ☐ ☐

10. You are forty-five but look ten years younger. Someone compliments you on your lovely hair and its youthful jet black colour. Are you more likely to say:
   a. 'Thank you' ☐ ☐
   b. 'It is the hair dye' ☐ ☐

	Yes	No

11. When you read your own CV, it looks:
    a. Partly like you ☐ ☐
    b. Absolutely like you ☐ ☐
    c. Neither ☐ ☐

12. You are the CEO of a company. Your company has just been awarded recognition by a trade journal for 'great contribution to sustainability'. They have sent you a mail asking you to come and receive it at a glittering function. You have no idea your company did this stuff. Will you:
    a. Reject the award ☐ ☐
    b. Ask the magazine to clarify the basis of selection, the jury and who were you compared with for the award ☐ ☐
    c. Send the head of PR to collect the award ☐ ☐

6

Seeking Help

Unfortunately many of us have been raised in a system that looks down upon admitting inadequacy. We are not supposed to say, 'I do not know'. Yet, as we grow in our careers, we just cannot know everything and cannot do everything by ourselves. We need help.

Asking for help is not that easy. Apart from the risk of facing refusal, sometimes it can be a matter of embarrassment in front of a colleague or a customer. The perception of losing face is so strong that sometimes we choose to look knowledgeable—with regrettable outcomes—rather than raise an alert, admit inadequacy and seek help.

In 1993, I was chief executive of Wipro's Global R&D. We had just landed a major contract from Tandem, a maker of fault tolerant computers. It required training sixty engineers in the United States for long periods of time. The customer signed the deal and left to take a flight to Mumbai.

Just then we learnt from the American consulate in Chennai that the visa request for the first set of engineers had been turned down. They were not convinced that the travel was indeed for training purposes. It was a major blow. The contract, earned with months of hard work, was going to evaporate into thin air, but what was worse, we would all look foolish in front of our customer who had relied on our total project management ability.

My boss, Dr Sridhar Mitta, called me to his room and suggested we immediately call the customer to notify him of the setback. Then he added, we might as well ask him for help to diffuse the crisis. That was so counter-intuitive, I thought. How could one possibly expose the customer to the many variables we weren't really on top of?

But I had great faith in Dr Mitta's counsel and, even though the prospect of an angry customer loomed large, we dialled his number. He was about to board the plane. He was very upset when we told him what had happened, even though it wasn't Wipro's fault. Dr Mitta asked him if he could help by going along with us to the American consulate to explain the situation and seek reconsideration. The customer stayed back and went along with us; we met the consular officers and his sheer presence and advocacy satisfied them beyond doubt that the visa requests were genuine.

Not only were the visas cleared, but we faced no further issues during the entire tenure of the project. The project took off because Dr Mitta sought help without hesitation and on time.

In the space below, recount examples from your professional life where you sought help from someone and for which you feel grateful.

What seems more appropriate in your case?

1. You are new to the organization. You have been feeling feverish for the last couple of days. Are you more likely or less likely to ask a colleague you have just met to introduce you to a local doctor?

2. You have just joined a new company and do not know your way around the office. Are you more likely or less likely to reach out to a colleague in the adjoining cubicle and ask if you could have lunch together?

3. You are unable to solve a crossword puzzle by yourself. The passenger seated next to you seems to be a friendly person who earlier said he too found crosswords interesting; but he is reading a magazine right now. Are you more likely or less likely to ask him for help with a word?

4. When you are lost in a city, do you feel stupid to ask a stranger for directions?

5. You are stuck in the middle of a project and it requires expertise from another group. You do not like the head of the group. He comes across as a chest beater in meetings. Are you more likely or less likely to leave aside the prejudice and walk across to his office?

6. You have taken over as the manager of a new high-end retail chain that had no previous presence in your city. A new location has been chosen in a neighbourhood that has mostly small shops and eateries. Are you more likely or less likely to go and meet the owners to make a personal acquaintance before starting the store?

7. You have just taken over as the tax consultant for a company. The man who did the job from the client side for twenty years is retiring next week. Are you more likely or less likely to call on him to congratulate him, wish him all the best and make a request to be available to you for future consultation if you got stuck somewhere?

8. You have just clinched a large deal. You have three quarters of the expertise needed to build the solution. The gap that you have is the sweet spot of another competing company. Are you more likely or less likely to go to them to explore a partnering arrangement?

9. You are the new boss of a large department and some people are resentful; there are a few, you have been told, who think you are under-qualified. Today, you are about to go to a meeting where numbers will be discussed. There is one item on the spread sheet that you cannot understand. It may not be anything major. Are you more likely or less likely to walk up to the dealing person and admit your ignorance saying, 'Somehow I am not able to get this, will you please help me understand why this number is what it is?'

10. There was a technical conversation in the last meeting you attended that simply went above your head. You did not want to interrupt the flow by asking too many questions. Are you more likely or less likely to call the young intern who was speaking at the meeting to help you understand what got discussed?

11. After the half hour of conversation with the intern are you more likely or less likely to thank him and suggest you take him out to lunch for being a good coach?

12. When colleagues at work get stuck with problems they cannot solve, are they more likely or less likely to peep in and seek your help?

The ability to seek help is an indication of self-confidence.

Many senior folks in large organizations feel extremely awkward to ask for help, particularly from peers and subordinates. But remember this, people who do ask for help at work are more likely to be asked to help by others. This becomes the foundation of a valuable network.

Sometimes help resides in the most unlikely places, like an ex-rival in the company or a tiny store down the street where you have opened business. People are more likely to help if they think you are humble. Quite often people in positions of authority forget to say thank you for help received.

7

Avoiding False Comparison

Everyone suffers from false comparison at one time or the other. The issue is how intense it is, how long it lasts and how often it recurs.

When I joined Wipro in 1988 as a mid-level manager, I thought the salary package offered to me was reasonable. Upon joining, it occurred to me that in Wipro, at my level, it was difficult to make one-to-one comparisons with others who were already there before me. To start with, practically everyone was an engineer and an MBA. I was not. Secondly, most of them had worked at Wipro for a long time. Now, here was a piece of complexity: not only did I not study engineering and management, but I started working at nineteen. As a result, those of my age in the system who had done engineering and then an MBA usually had four to five years *less* work experience than I did.

From my point of view, I had more work experience, and from the system's point of view, they were better qualified. Knowing specific details of the money my peers made was therefore neither simple, nor did the matter greatly interest me. What did, however, was the grade they were in.

Wipro being a young and competitive company, people fretted when someone moved to a higher grade six months sooner than others. When I joined Wipro, I was a fairly familiar name in the industry because I used to write a column in *Dataquest* magazine. This, along with my greater years of experience, told me (not unreasonably) that I should have been taken in at a higher grade.

The good thing was that this was a fleeting feeling and did not get me obsessed at any stage. Until, of course, my peers started moving into the next higher grade ahead of me.

Two of my MindTree co-founders and I were all born within weeks of each other in 1957. All three of us were at Wipro together and they moved to a higher grade before I did. S. Janakiraman had done his MTech at IIT and then joined Wipro from the campus. He was no. 3 in the R&D department.

Krishna Kumar was an engineer and a management graduate from XLRI and was a regional sales head. I started feeling neglected in comparison.

That feeling did not last long, luckily, because I soon got an opportunity to start Wipro's businesses from the ground up in the US and it submerged all mental comparisons.

Then something funny happened: I got the next two promotions a little ahead of them and eventually, when we started MindTree, we were at the same level. All this was an up and down, a bob you may say, over a period of ten years. As I look back, the fleeting comparisons were meaningless and distracting.

> The question should not be why so and so gets a higher salary than me or gets promoted before I do. The question should be, am I being treated fairly for the work I do and the tangible value I bring to the organization—not just for my past experience or education?

If the answer is no, a discussion is in order. Good companies these days have authentic third-party surveys to create compensation models that are fair and reasonable. Having said that, life is not always reasonable. But the solution is not in making persistent comparisons—mostly they are false.

False comparisons are made not just within the same organization or based purely on professional considerations. Many of us keep comparing ourselves with a friend left behind two decades ago who might have chosen an altogether different career trajectory. One probably went into research and the other became a salesman. The material outcome of the countless choices each person made over the decades becomes vastly different. But along the way, we make comparisons between how much who has made. It leaves a person feeling invariably poorer, materially or mentally—usually both. The sooner I become my own benchmark, the better it is for my mental equilibrium and for my capacity to focus on what can get me ahead, not what can get me at par.

In the space below, please write a short essay to yourself on making the right comparisons and making false comparisons. Who do you usually compare yourself with and for what?

Similarly, are there other examples around you that make for an interesting recollection?

According to you, which of the following may be false comparisons? Cross out the false ones.

1. Compensation of a friend who had once studied engineering with you
2. Comparative roles and responsibilities
3. Revenue impact you make versus someone else
4. How much annuity sales another sales manager has inherited
5. Net take-home pay of others in the same grade
6. Gross pay of others in the same grade
7. Schools your respective children go to
8. How well your kids sleep at night
9. Grades of other people's children
10. How much time you have spent with your kids this month
11. What you have read lately and what your friend has read
12. What new sport your colleague is excelling in
13. How much time you are giving to a new sport you learnt last year
14. Who is running marathons on company time
15. How many days are you working out in a month
16. Who spends how much time in the cafeteria
17. When did you last watch a movie in a theatre with your best buddy
18. Who is sucking up to the boss
19. When did you buy something for your spouse that made her smile
20. What are your plans for getting a great customer win next year
21. What car is your enemy driving
22. Did you read a story to your child last week
23. Someone else's spend on beauty
24. Your weight and someone else's
25. Work practices of people doing admirably well

8

A Reasonable View of the Future

During the height of the financial meltdown in Greece and Spain in 2011, there was widespread talk on how this might lead to a larger crisis and what roles Germany and France could play to prevent a pan-Europe meltdown. The then chief of the International Monetary Fund, Dominique Strauss-Kahn, was shuttling between Europe and the US and he, it was believed, could lead everyone out of the crisis. There was speculation that Germany and France would give Greece and Spain large bailout packages to arrest the spread of the economic crisis. Consequently, many of their own citizens were alarmed and unhappy.

This was the larger picture when I boarded a taxi in Cologne, Germany. As is my habit when I ride a taxi in a new country, I started chatting with the German driver and asked him his opinion on the economic scenario and the overall sense of gloom.

'It is a matter of worry for those people who have too much money in the bank,' he replied, keeping his eyes on the road ahead.

His unusual reply surprised me and I prodded for more. 'Look,' he said, 'economic meltdown or not, people will eat, go to the church, make love, have babies, see a doctor, send children to school. You will come again to Germany. I will drive this taxi. I will take people like you from one place to the other. These simple things won't change and life will go on.'

This was irrefutable logic and what I would call a reasonable view of the future.

We are in 2012 now. Greece and Spain are still very much around, as are France and Germany. Strauss-Kahn has been in and out of trouble over allegations that he forced a hotel maid into having sex. He had to quit the IMF and lost a run-up to the French presidency.

Yes, there will always be wars, a currency volatility that will shake everyone, a large merger and acquisition, a tsunami, and something else that you didn't see coming. Yet, people not only survive, but by and large hard-working people do make it.

Good people have a reasonable view of themselves, their world and the world around them. They are neither unduly pessimistic, nor do they suffer from what is termed 'irrational exuberance'.

If someone has a persistently gloomy outlook on their workplace, their boss and colleagues, it is time to see a physician. One in five people suffer from serious mental health issues like depression that need to be addressed just like we take on diabetes or hypertension. Our personal world view and professional world view are seldom at variance with each other. Optimism moves fluidly in and out of our lives—it seldom distinguishes between what may be personal and professional.

Another fact of life is that there are bound to be the occasional bad times in everyone's life. But neither bad times nor good times last forever. Bad times must be used to prepare for good times, and vice versa.

In the facing page trace your entire lifespan so far, highlighting each part that you think witnessed a strongly positive or a negative event—and then step back to consider the view in its totality as if you are looking at a drawing depicting someone else's life story.

THIS IS THE PICTURE OF MY LIFE SO FAR

9

Affective Regard

List below the names of five professionals you deeply admire for what they have achieved for themselves and for others. These five may be from your workplace or your extended circle of acquaintances, or may even include people you've never met but admire tremendously.

1.

2.

3.

4.

5.

Now please list any three qualities for every individual you admire that got them to your list in the space below:

1.
a)
b)
c)

2.
a)
b)
c)

3.
a)
b)
c)

4.
a)
b)
c)

5.
a)
b)
c)

Is there a certain pattern, a common thread emerging as you look at your five most-admired professionals?

Of the fifteen qualities you listed for the five great professionals (some qualities would be common of course), how many times did you list accumulated personal wealth of the professional as the quality that has earned your respect?

Money has two distinctive usages. It has a consumptive value for us and it can have a regenerative value as well.

The consumptive value of money is about satisfying our personal wants and needs: eating out, buying an expensive garment or a good watch, going on a nice holiday. We all need these in order to feel good about ourselves and accumulate a sense of well-being.

At the same time, lasting happiness is a function of putting money to work for us: for example, building a house that could be an asset during old age or become the proverbial nest egg; investing some money to build a small business; or, for that matter, earning in order to build something useful for other people in our lives.

The two kinds of usage are very different in their ability to make us happy. They are intrinsically different from each other. The happiness I receive from buying a mango and eating it and the joy of planting a mango tree that will give fruit someday are entirely different. Only those who have done the latter can appreciate the difference.

Having an adequate source of money to take care of both consumptive needs and regenerative needs is necessary in life. However, the regenerative use of money is not guaranteed just because one has money. It requires a very different kind of thinking.

The problem with consumption is that it can never satisfy anyone indefinitely. While we all must consume in order to feel good, one must know its limited power to make us happy.

A profession is not just a means to earn money; it is something that literally holds us, it defines who we are.

That is why when someone asks who we are, we say I am a doctor, I am an engineer, I am a lawyer or I am a physical fitness teacher. Since our profession defines our very existence, gives us a large portion of our self-identity, it requires us to build what we term 'affective regard' for the profession.

> Real professional success is a function of giving back to the profession more than we take out of it.

We admire rich doctors and engineers and lawyers. But the ones we revere and remember are those who have given back to their professions.

This giving back can be done in many ways. When I read a paper at a conference, I am sharing my knowledge. When I join an industry group and devote personal time to it, I am helping build an institution. When I spend planned time with young interns at my workplace, I am building a legacy. When I give away a part of my savings to start a new business or donate it to charity, I am creating a regenerative use of my professional income.

Each of these creates the most valuable asset: peer recognition. It comes slowly and builds gradually but, in the end, only this and nothing else creates reputation capital for all of us.

List below a few things you could do to make your profession richer, more alive, and more respected in the eyes of society.

How much time will you devote to these things? What is needed to sustain your giving over time?

10

Deep Listening

Now, there are three personal exercises I want you to undertake. These are simple but promise to be potentially very beneficial for you.

Please do the three exercises today, tomorrow and the day after, at approximately the same time.

Each exercise will take about half an hour.

For today, please read and complete only the one exercise meant for today. **Do not read up now on what is meant for tomorrow and the day after.**

The three exercises are part of a series of self-discovery. Just do as suggested and do not try to attach any meaning or draw any conclusions from the individual exercises as you go along. Just be one with the process.

Here is an important requirement: please choose a relatively quiet location where you will not be interrupted by anyone.

It is now time to start today's exercise.

Exercise 1

This exercise needs you to stay quiet in one place for ten minutes. Please time yourself with the alarm in your cell phone and read the following instructions carefully.

The first step is to close your eyes. Then take a deep breath, exhale fully and settle down. Breathe easy. Calm your mind. Watch your thoughts come and go. Do not focus on any one thought and do not try to stop any.

After a few seconds, shift your attention gently to listening to the various sounds around you. Some may originate from near you, some from farther away. Identify the sounds and keep noting the unique ones.

This is the exercise. After you have completed ten minutes of listening to the various sounds, gently, very gently, open your eyes. Stay quiet for a couple of minutes and then go to the next page.

You are now ready to start today's exercise.

WHAT DID I HEAR?

In the space below, please list all the sounds you identified. The more sounds you have heard, the better. Some may have come from near you and some from far away. Some may be subtle and some obvious.

- —
- —
- —
- —
- —
- —
- —
- —
- —
- —
- —
- —
- —
- —
- —
- —

After writing out the list above, please take a five-minute rest without getting up. After five minutes, please turn the page.

This exercise requires you to repeat exactly what you just did.

But before you start, please read the following lines carefully again.

Please time yourself with the alarm in your cell phone for a quiet exercise in one place for ten minutes. The next step is to close your eyes. Take a deep breath and then try and breathe easy.

Calm your mind.

Watch your thoughts come and go.

Do not focus on any one thought and do not try to stop any.

After a few seconds, shift your attention gently to listening to the various sounds around you. Some would be coming from near you, some from farther away. Some may be the same sounds you heard before and some very new ones.

Please identify the sounds and keep noting the unique ones.

This is the exercise. After you have completed ten minutes of listening to the various sounds and the alarm rings, gently, very gently, open your eyes.

Please stay quiet for a couple of minutes and then go to the next page.

WHAT DID I HEAR NOW?

Please list a few sounds that you may have missed the first time around.

Please do not write down any that you had already listed after the first part of the exercise.

—

—

—

—

—

—

—

—

—

—

—

—

WHAT REALLY HAPPENED JUST NOW?

What you just did was a simple but interesting exercise.

A pleasant side effect many experience as part of this exercise is the slowing of breath. Some people even nod off for a few seconds. That of course is not the idea behind the exercise, even though you may experience a pleasant sense of calm. The idea is to be aware and remain awake.

Between the first time and the second, you listened more deeply. You observed sounds. Many of the sounds were there around you even during the first exercise but you did not notice them at all then. You noticed them only as you calmed down further.

Most people miss out the sound of the air conditioner or the ceiling fan and the sound of their own breathing the first time. Some miss the distinctive difference between the very different sounds of breathing in and breathing out. Did you? Did you hear your own heartbeat?

> There are six things in common to every professional: a maximum available time of twenty-four hours in a day, and the same five senses: hearing, seeing, smelling, taste and touch.
>
> Part of being a good professional is the ability to utilize time well, and to use one's five senses as effectively as possible.

In the two-step exercise you just did, you listened and then you listened at some more depth.

Please stop reading now and take a break until tomorrow.

Exercise 2

Welcome back!

Since you are now familiar with the overall process, today's exercise should be even more interesting and enjoyable.

You may please proceed now.

In the page overleaf, write down, in as much detail as possible, your happiest moment in life.

Observe it happen all over again, slowly, frame by frame.

Remember to recall your entry point, the location, the cast, the conversations, the silent spaces, the changes . . . and your exit from the moment, from your memory.

Do not go to the next page until you have completed writing.

MY HAPPIEST MOMENT IN LIFE

Please go back and read what you have written and see if you have missed anything. You may add notes to the narrative in the space below.

Please close the workbook now and reflect on the work you've done until now.

Go forward only tomorrow.

Exercise 3

Welcome back!

Today, we will go deeper into the listening process.

Please read the instructions below:

Sit comfortably in a very quiet place where you may not be interrupted. Today is not about listening to sounds. It will be about listening to feelings.

For this, you will need to breathe gently for some time; observe your breathing until you find it easy. The real exercise is about observing your whole body gently, slowly, keeping your eyes closed all the while.

For each step I list below, always stop for a few seconds. Be unhurried and then gently move to the next.

You may proceed to the next page and start now.

Start from your toes, observe them, and imagine them as if you are seeing them.

Gently proceed to the soles of the feet and again observe them the same way.

Then the ankles, the calf muscles, the knees, the thighs, the pelvic region.

Then the stomach, the chest, the lower back, the middle back, the upper back.

Now the fingers of both hands, the palms, the wrists, the forearms, the upper arms, the shoulders, the neck, the chin, the jaws, the nose, the cheeks, the eyes, the forehead, the top of the head, the back of the head.

At each step, be aware of the position, observe whatever you feel—sometimes a twitch, sometimes nothing at all.

After moving from your toes to the head, gently go down in the reverse order.

Noting each body part you previously came by, observe the part and whatever feeling may be there for a few seconds and keep moving along till you reach your toes again.

Note every twitch, every pressure and every small sensation. Observe and gently move on.

Repeat the process for as long as you want.

When you have completed at least six rounds of going up and down, gently open your eyes without disturbing your posture.

> Our ability to observe our thoughts, feelings and actions directly impacts our capacity of self-observation.
> Great professionals are self-observant.

11

Reining in
Reaction

What is the most important tool of any professional? Without an iota of doubt, it is the human brain.

How much do we understand how our own brain works? Probably not much, in the case of most people. If that is so, are we a bunch of people yielding a tool whose use we do not know but use it nonetheless? That is a scary thought, isn't it?

For a moment, imagine that you do not know how a drill works; should you be using it? Or you do not know how to drive well; would you drive on the highway? Unfortunately, Mother Nature does not ship us with a user's manual. That is why we must pay great attention to this fascinating organ called the human brain.

In particular, we will talk about two parts of the brain: the amygdala and the neo-cortex. Our reaction to situations and people are managed by these two.

The amygdala is situated at the base of the brain; in many ways, it is a mini-brain in itself. Sometimes called the primitive brain, the amygdala develops fully even as we are in the mother's womb, and does not change during our lifetime. The rest of the brain, much larger, keeps growing after birth and keeps 'learning' and 'remembering' things. But our most essential instructions are pre-programmed in the amygdala.

These are the instructions vital for survival. The amygdala alerts us to imminent danger and controls our flight-or-fight responses. It does not understand words and numbers because these were created by humans. Instead, it rapidly processes information that is based on shape, size, colour and movement. Given the slightest possibility of danger to life, it rapidly receives the information and releases emergency instructions to all parts of the body. That is what makes you step back 'instinctively' when you see a coiled something lying in a dark alley, even before your brain has had time to understand what it is—a rope: the amygdala is not taking any chances. Just look at what happened to you this very moment! When you read the previous sentence, your brain alerted you at once about what the coiled something in a dark alley might be. How long did that take?

The amygdala controls our basic instincts. It triggers emotions. The word 'emotion' has its origin in Latin; it means, feelings that *move* us. The amygdala also tells us to care for our babies. In mammals, the amygdala is large. If it is removed surgically, an animal does not care for its offspring any more.

So, the amygdala helps me by simulating fear. Fear is a useful emotion; it helps us save ourselves. Then there is anger; it is meant to ward off danger. That is why fear and anger are present in a dog, a dolphin, a crow—and in us.

But sometimes, the amygdala overreacts. Mother Nature has designed it that way. She rather errs on the side of safety. But this can cause some really dangerous consequences.

Daniel Goleman, author of the book *Emotional Intelligence*, drives home the danger of an overactive amygdala through the story of a father who shot his daughter dead. The parents were returning home at 1.00 a.m. and their teenage daughter, who wasn't expected back that night, tried to surprise them by jumping out of a cupboard. The father thought she was an intruder, drew his gun and shot her. In moments like these, the amygdala takes over all functions of the brain and directs behaviour because it interprets the situation as a life-and-death issue.

Now let us go back to the 'coiled something in the dark alley' example. When the amygdala reacts and you jump back, the frontal part of the brain, the rational brain, begins to interpret the object in an overall context and tells every other organ to relax because it is not a serpent but a rope. You laugh at your own stupidity but again thank God that it wasn't the real thing—it is always good to be careful.

So, the amygdala is protective; it takes no chances, it rushes adrenalin into the bloodstream so that you can run, hit back, do whatever you need to protect yourself. But uncontrolled, not tempered by reason, it can create an 'emotional hijack'. That is how we get uncontrollably angry sometimes and then, later on, regret it. Emotional hijack causes many of the murders that are not premeditated. This includes parents killing their own children when they interpret a child's act as defiance.

Emotional hijack also causes far-reaching, consequential damage, ranging from the Jallianwala Bagh massacre undertaken by General Dyer to the excesses of the three policemen who beat up Rodney King in Los Angeles. Both these instances illustrate how fear and anger in excess can have damaging consequences. Both General Dyer and the policemen in Los Angeles were professionally trained but failed to rein in their reaction. Every professional, from a policeman to a doctor to a teacher, can come under extreme pressure and in each case experience an emotional hijack, though usually not as extreme and damaging as the two examples cited.

A real professional is one who can take the pressure, who does not let the situation take control over the self and lead to regrettable circumstances.

What are you most likely to choose as an option in the following situations?

1. You see a child hit by a speeding motorist on the road; the child is crying loudly. Would you:
   a. Run and pick up the child
   b. Do not risk the above but call the police immediately
   c. Take a big stone and hurl it at the motorist so that he is forced to stop

2. An idiot in your organization has hit the 'Reply All' button on a spam mail by another dim-witted colleague who had no business venting publicly. Would you:
   a. Send a fitting reply to the replier
   b. Curse them
   c. Delete the mail

3. An irate customer who has been on hold for thirty minutes—or so she claims—is on the line and you have to again, unfortunately, keep her on hold because you need to pull her record; she uses a cuss word. Would you:
   a. Disconnect
   b. Give her a firm reply and ask her to stop doing that
   c. Ignore it for the time being

4. Your neighbour comes in really upset and tells you that your son has used a really bad word while talking to his teenage daughter. Your son is standing in front of you. Are you most likely to:
   a. Challenge the neighbour to prove what he is saying
   b. Slap the son for what he has most probably done
   c. Tell the neighbour that you will need to speak to your son privately

5. A colleague is going overboard in telling the entire office at the cafeteria how your department has created all the mess that his staff must now clean up. Would you:
   a. Give him a cold stare, go to his boss and complain
   b. Take no nonsense and give him an earful
   c. Tell him that it is not a fair statement and that you two should meet later that afternoon and have a word

6. A rude customer keeps you waiting for a good one hour only to show his power to his staff and then gives you a dressing down for a solvable problem your people have unwittingly created. Would you:
   a. Take no such nonsense and stand up for your people
   b. Listen to him, go out, confer with your people and write him a mail
   c. Apologize because the customer is always right

7. A drunken person is pestering a young lady in a late night train. No one is coming to her rescue. Would you:
   a. Intervene loudly, drawing everyone's attention
   b. Ask the lady if she needs help
   c. Look the other way

8. A local journalist has written a damaging story about you in the daily tabloid. Would you:
   a. Talk to your lawyer
   b. Ask your colleague in corporate relations to take up the matter
   c. Send out an immediate disclaimer to the editor

9. Your boss has screamed at you for no fault of yours behind closed doors. The guy is going through a mid-life crisis and is taking it out on you. Would you:

   a. Tell him to find someone else to vent on

   b. Give him a glass of water and ask him to sit down first

   c. Give him tit for tat

10. An anonymous complainer has written a really obnoxious letter about you to your CEO and it has come to your notice. You know nothing may happen but you are reasonably sure of who might have done it. Would you:

    a. Ignore the episode

    b. Confront the suspect

    c. Check if you might have done something that allows someone else to interpret your action wrongly

Now, take a few minutes to write down in the space below an instance of someone unable to rein in reaction under pressure, your opinion on what could have caused it and how you might have handled the situation better.

12

Using Your Own Two Hands

One day, hurtling through a New York City tunnel aboard a subway train, I found myself asking a strange question: 'What would I do if the world of business came to a dead halt?'

That would mean real estate would crash as well and so would the stock market; other than two houses I owned at the time and the MindTree stocks, I had nothing. Even though the houses and the stocks were worth more than many people had, if the business world came to an end, the houses would have no takers and the stocks could plummet to nothing. What would then happen to me? How would I live?

I do not know how to till the soil; I have never done it. That ruled out farming, growing something to eat myself and trading the surplus. I do not have the skills to go and catch fish in the ocean. I cannot make medicine out of herbs or stitch up an open wound for someone. I cannot sing to save my life, nor can I make toys or cook for others. A cup of tea and an omelette I can manage but I cannot toss a pizza into a brick oven.

I was looking desperately for something useful that I can do with my own two hands to create value. That would never go out of demand even if the modern-day economy dominated by white-collar workers collapsed.

Then I remembered: I know how to polish shoes. In fact, I love to polish shoes. I learnt how to do it as a boy and even today I love it and I still polish my own shoes.

I smiled to myself. I could sit someplace where people came and went, like in a subway station or outside, near the square, and polish their shoes. I suddenly felt so much better.

Then the train came out of the tunnel.

Make a list of all the things you do well with your own hands. Write them down as they come to your mind.

1.

2.

3.

4.

5.

6.

7.

8.

9.

10.

Now, choose three of the ten things above that you think you're best at.

Assign a total of 25 points that you may distribute among these three skills.

Points

1.

2.

3.

You listed three things you love doing the most in the previous exercise. Please write them again below.

1.

2.

3.

Can you now put down the date you last did these things against each one?

Date

1.

2.

3.

Now, think about the following situations:

1. Your department is winding up. What other department would readily want your services?

2. Your company is closing down. What work could you do in another?

3. Your industry itself is no more. What do you see yourself doing for a living now?

List some names against each of the following categories:

Category 1: List three senior people in your organization outside your department who really like you and know about your work.

–

–

–

Category 2: List two people outside your company/organization who admire your work.

–

–

Category 3: Name one person outside your industry who has a good understanding of and admiration for your work. Would the individual respond to your mail to write a recommendation for you?

–

Now reflect on the following:

For the people in category 1, ask yourself: when was the last time that you met over coffee?

For category 2, when was the last that you called on them, had a meal together and discussed work?

For category 3, when was it last that you said something like, 'Please let me know how I can be of any use to you; all you have to do is ask, I would love to be of help'?

13

Being Proactive

Two of my colleagues met me the other day to ask if I would be available to meet with a very senior person visiting from one of MindTree's top five customers. As is the process, they briefed me about the state of the relationship, the customer's business situation and the organization structure—and told me all about the importance of the visit for us.

At the end of the briefing, I asked them the following question: 'Imagine I just met the visitor at an international airport and we just got to know each other for the very first time, and were pleasantly surprised to know that our two companies did business with each other. What, in the ensuing half hour, would we be talking to each other about?'

My colleagues were baffled. They had done the so-called research very well but all the inputs were about the past.

> When professionals meet, they seek to explore the future and this requires being proactive.

Being proactive in this case is all about stepping into the shoes of the customer, about imagining things from the other person's perspective. This opens up an entirely new set of possibilities.

When the customer arrived, we did not discuss the software services that we provide to his company. That is well taken care of from both sides by very competent people.

The customer spoke to me about his new chief executive who wanted to double their business in the next decade but without increasing their company's present carbon footprint.

So, we spoke to each other about sustainability and the result was a deeper, more memorable tie between two individuals.

In today's world, there is abundance of everything. In a world where there is abundance, memorability is at a premium. The customer in this case must be coming across three, four, or five people like me every week as he flies in and out of continents. Why and how would he remember me a few months from now?

That question begs a conversation about proactivity above all else.

Being proactive is a magical way of creating the future.

Here are fifty questions for you. Tick the ones that best describe your own self in most situations. Think carefully before you tick. Look for evidence in your mind before you rate yourself.

1. When I make eye contact with someone, I smile.
2. When I get out of bed, I have an idea of how I am going to make my day work.
3. I remember other people's birthdays.
4. I don't wait for people to wish me first.
5. I keep a to-do list.
6. I like the idea of making a plan.
7. I ask myself a lot of questions before I jump into a task.
8. I look for resources around me and seek help when needed.
9. I thank people when they are not expecting to be thanked.
10. I check out the menu of a restaurant online before landing up there.
11. I immediately reach out to customers for clarity when I do not understand their requirements.
12. I ask for feedback on how I can do my work better.
13. I like to learn new things outside of my work.
14. I say sorry as soon as I realize I have made a mistake.
15. I like preventing problems rather than solving problems.
16. I do not neglect the 'important-but-not-urgent' tasks.
17. My friends come to me to seek help and advice.
18. If I see a task as repetitive, I try and see how it can be automated.
19. I go back to my customers and check if my product or service has met their expectations.
20. I am the one more likely to invite a colleague to share lunch.
21. I listen well to people during lunch conversations.
22. I learn on my own.
23. I ask people to teach me things.
24. I have used personal time to attend professional training on my own.
25. I ask my supervisor for help before I run into trouble.

26. I often volunteer to my supervisor to help out.
27. I try to create expertise outside my work group in our partner organizations.
28. I am happy to share my knowledge at work with my colleagues.
29. I use the Internet actively for learning to stay ahead.
30. I help out at home without being asked to.
31. I like making things with my own hands.
32. I can sense people's moods and feelings.
33. I consciously think of how I could do things better.
34. I think of what may or can go wrong with things around me.
35. I alert people to problems.
36. I promptly alert people to mistakes on my part.
37. I speak to my customers and suppliers without their reaching out to me for something.
38. I look for lessons from every assignment that I complete.
39. I like to do research about people and companies even before I may need it.
40. I regularly read professional literature.
41. I help strangers if I think they are in need of anything.
42. I like to think about how things around me could be improved.
43. If I have a suggestion, I look for a box.
44. I return to see if my suggestion has been accepted.
45. I am never late for meetings.
46. I invariably read up before attending a meeting.
47. I participate actively in meetings and put forth my views.
48. People call me to join their groups when they are trying to solve a problem.
49. I volunteer time outside work.
50. I mentor someone at work.

> Proactive individuals are empathetic, analytical and action-oriented. They seldom need supervision. They are less likely to get into situations against their will. They can say no without being offensive.

14

Taking Charge: Handling Difficult Situations

Have you ever been in a chaotic situation, like in front of an airline desk after a flight cancellation with other jostling, angry passengers like yourself? Or at a hospital counter with people in a state of confusion when a patient has just been wheeled in? Or maybe someplace else like a government office where you are running from pillar to post trying to get something done?

When you think of such situations, the one single thought that was probably running through your mind was: Who is in charge here? Every once one a while, we all encounter that question.

Sometimes, it is a helpless feeling. Sometimes, it is an angry feeing. Most of the time, it is a statement of prayer. Then the situation changes and in comes the deliverer.

A man or a woman arrives, telling the impatient group of anxious, confused and angry people something like, 'Please give me a few minutes, I am here to help you, just be patient.' The tension begins to go away, the anger dissipates and life soon returns to normal. You feel relieved that someone is now in charge.

> Taking charge is a critical aspect of professional duty.

However, in most professional situations, beyond the rulebook, taking charge is the voluntary act of a professional who rises to the occasion. Sometimes the act of taking charge may even entail a fairly high personal risk.

In the space below, can you recount a personal or professional incident involving a difficult situation in which you took charge?

Can you recall a situation in which someone else—a doctor, a policeman, a teacher or a bystander—took charge, and you really admired the individual for handling the situation?

WHAT IS NEEDED TO TAKE CHARGE?

- Empathy
- Courage
- Risk-taking
- Listening
- Intuitive Thinking
- Restraint
- Communicating Intent
- Communication Skills
- Negotiation Skills
- Objection Handling
- Prioritizing
- Decision-making
- Getting Closure
- Handing Back Control
- Letting Go
- Rallying Support
- Sense-making
- Seeking Help
- Thanking
- Notifying Progress
- Self-confidence
- Heroism
- Altruism

Please think back to the two incidents you have just written about. How many of these aspects came into play in each?

15

A Personal Vision

In the two boxes below, paste two photographs that you think show you at your best. Choose one from ten years ago and one that is very recent:

Year of this picture

....

Year of this picture

....

Now please look at the two photographs together. What are the similarities that you see, and what are the changes? How have you changed in the photographs in ways that are evident?

In what other ways have you changed that are not depicted in the pictures?

List below the conscious professional investments you have made in the intervening period between the times the two pictures were taken.

1. These are three books I read that changed me in some fundamental ways.

    _

    _

    _

2. These are three of my most memorable trips, and these are the years each took place.

    _

    _

    _

3. These are three people I met in the last ten years who have left a lasting impression on mc and hcrc arc the reasons why.

    _

    _

    _

4. Here is my one big assignment during this period that made me feel I have really grown up in a personal and professional sense.

5. Here is a sport or a physical activity I took up that I have been putting to good use.

6. This is something I gave back, in whatever form, to someone beyond my usual circle that made me really feel good about myself.

7. This is what I saw my doctor for and this is an advice I have taken very seriously since then.

8. These are the material, long-term assets I created during this time.

9. Here is what I did to help myself spiritually.

10. Here are three friends I met after a really long break.

    –

    –

    –

11. Here is what I learnt in my profession that makes me more employable in the future.

12. Here are three bad habits I had ten years ago which I no longer do.

    –

    –

    –

13. Here is a new habit (good or bad) that I have picked up along the way.

14. Here are my three customers or clients to whom I have made a big difference.

    –

    –

    –

Please take a break until tomorrow at this point. Do not turn the page now.

Welcome back!

Please go back now and read your answers to the fourteen questions you reflected on yesterday.

These pretty much define who you are today and how you have grown from who you were a decade ago.

After you have read them, please proceed to the next question.

15. Here are the three things in life that I must accomplish, that are still left for me to do, come what may.

    –

    –

    –

16

Managing Your Time Right

Effective time management is key to any professional's success.

In the book *The 7 Habits of Highly Effective People*, Steven Covey introduced the Four Quadrants theory. He divided workplace activities into four categories, defined along the axes of urgency and importance.

	URGENT	NOT URGENT
IMPORTANT	I	II
NOT IMPORTANT	III	IV

Activities in the first quadrant include crises and deadline-driven projects; in the second quadrant are such long-term activities as planning, capability improvement, relationship building and recognizing new opportunities; in the third quadrant are workplace duties such as meetings, reports, e-mails and things that need immediate attention; while the fourth quadrant covers trivia, 'time wasters', and mails and phone calls that are not urgent.

Obviously, the most important quadrant is the second, but most of our time is spent in dealing with activities in the first and third quadrants, and a fair bit of the workday is often wasted in activities of the fourth quadrant.

Now, answer these questions about your workplace time management.

1. Which quadrant do I primarily live in?

2. What are my recurring time wasters?

3. What should I start doing to manage my time better?

4. What should I stop doing to manage my time better?

17

Saying No

The ability to say 'No' is an important part of effective time management.

Answer this question for yourself:

Can I say 'No' if I need to?

If the answer is 'Yes' please go on to the next page.

If the answer is 'No', please read the note below from Wikihow:

> Unproductive activities, time wasting or the invitation to do unlawful things at the workplace are not uncommon at all. Many people learn to deal with these by trial and error, or are lucky to be mentored right. For some of us, saying no to any unreasonable request is inherently difficult. This is not just at the workplace, but also true in our day-to-day life. We end up giving in and then regret it. The root of this may be inside the person giving in, sometimes it can be an outcome of low self-confidence. It is necessary to learn about this and self-correct. If you still find it difficult, it may be good to see a counsellor.

Wikihow has an eight-step guideline to show you how to say no. Do visit www.wikihow.com/Say-No-Respectfully for detailed explanations of each. The eight steps are:

- Listen to the request respectfully. Do not interrupt the speaker.
- Phrase your 'no' as simply as possible.
- Transfer ownership of your refusal to something else.
- Try to remain non-confrontational.
- Don't feel obligated to explain.
- Explain simply, and only if you wish to do so.
- Stand firm.
- Keep in mind that it's your time they are requesting for and you have a choice.

Saying 'No' when needed is an important professional requirement.

It does sometimes result in difficult situations with a co-worker, a customer or, worse, your own boss. But, overall, by saying 'No' you show others that they should not take you for granted. More important, you are able to take a definitive position with your own self. You will be surprised how, when done in the right measure, it can build your self-confidence. Do know that your response must be reasoned. Ask yourself each time, before and after saying 'No', how reasonable your response was, and be open to feedback.

List below three occasions in the last one year when you have said no and your assertion has turned out positively for yourself.

1.

2.

3.

Remember, you do not *have* to say yes to any of these . . .

1. A invitation to drinks from your boss
2. Unnecessary travel
3. A meeting from which you will have no learning nor have anything to contribute
4. You have your own work overdue and unfinished; someone else is asking for help
5. Someone is asking you for a loan at the workplace and you would really rather not give it
6. A co-worker you do not know well is asking you to be a referee
7. A head hunter enticing you when you are not looking for a change says, 'At least come and attend the interview'
8. Someone is giving you a task that you are not trained for
9. A customer is asking you to accept a conference call on your wife's birthday, when you're on leave
10. A supplier has brought you a gift
11. You are really not feeling well at all and your boss wants you to stay late
12. A stranger is asking you to give them a lift
13. A married co-worker is asking you to come home for a drink and suggestively says there would be no one else there
14. The boss is asking for a sexual favour when you are asking for a raise
15. Your friend working for a competitor is asking for friendly inside information
16. Your interviewer is asking you for the organizational chart of your current company
17. Your future employer is asking you for a copy of the existing company's business plan
18. Your customer is asking for a bribe
19. Your co-workers want you to throw a party at their favourite restaurant which you feel is beyond your means

20. Your co-worker is asking you to swipe her card next morning because she may come late

21. Someone wants you to do something against the rule book that you would not do for yourself

22. Your boss asks you to download someone else's intellectual property and tells you nothing will happen

23. A very persuasive, attractive, upwardly mobile co-worker is asking you to change your holiday plans because he/she needs to take off during the exact same days

24. A close associate is asking for an overnight loan from the office cash; you know he will pay it back—you are 99.9 per cent assured

25. Your customer is forcing a deadline on you to impress his new boss at work; you know it is an impossible deadline that is unfair to your own people

For all you know, the other person is not going to be offended if you said no; he/she might be just flying a kite or simply testing you out. In any case, each of the above requests is unreasonable and is sometimes an unprofessional demand.

18

The Power of Networking

Each one of us is more powerful than we think because we are as powerful as our network is.

It is amazing how connected we are with people, some of them far more powerful and knowledgeable than us. These people in turn have trusted relationships with others like us. Together, we have a web of relationships. If we cultivate them proactively, we will soon see a great professional network that works for us.

In the world of the knowledge worker, we talk about three kinds of people: mavens, connectors and evangelists.

A **maven** is someone who is both a consumer and a producer of knowledge. This is the typical individual contributor: the medical intern, the entry-level software engineer, the architect, or the young lawyer.

Mavens are invariably connected to a more experienced set of people and we call them **connectors**.

A connector's primary competence is in creating and maintaining relationships among many mavens. So, a maven is connected to a connector and through that person the maven may get connected to other mavens and trade knowledge with them. Therefore, the connector is a force multiplier.

Imagine I am a general physician. I am connected to a specialist. This specialist in turn knows many others like me. So if I seek help, in an instant, my connector can provide me trusted access to many mavens like myself that I do not know.

But connectors can do even better.

Think of a connector who not only knows mavens like me but knows a super-specialist, someone with great professional standing: that individual is who we will call an **evangelist**. An evangelist is often the last word in any given branch of knowledge-work. This person may in turn be connected with other evangelists who have their own set of connectors and, through them, with many mavens.

When you think of a structure like this, suddenly you see that you are like a star in a constellation in the professional sky.

Three things become huge differentiators to such a networked professional. He/she consciously asks: Who is my connector? How actively am I invested in building a professional relationship of give and take with that connector? Finally, how great are the evangelists that my connector is connected to?

> In today's world, it is seldom the individual knowledge of a maven that can make a person differentiated and powerful; quite often it is this network of which the individual is a node.

While the above idea is not difficult to understand, most people do not understand something very critical: we should use and not misuse the network. Here are a few tips on how to make you as powerful as your professional network:

- Your connector or evangelist may not be in your line of hierarchy. They need not be your boss and boss's boss.
- Know who they are and be visible to them by your work and willingness to contribute.
- Volunteer to help your connector whenever you can. Volunteer to take up a quick research, validate an idea, run an errand; take a small load off the connector's shoulder every now and then. Do all this without being asked. In short, be available and willing, and create value without expectations or creating a sense of obligation.
- Be visible to a set of evangelists by virtue of the professional work you do. A few evangelists must know who you are, and how good you are. Do have a look at the diagram on the facing page to see how just one such network helps me in real life as an example.
- Know that this is not about having your résumé on LinkedIn. We are talking about creating, nurturing and benefiting from what may become an organic, respectful, value-creating network of professionals for an entire lifetime.

SUBROTO BAGCHI AS MAVEN

In many ways, I am a maven. I know a connector named Dr Thimappa Hegde who is a great neurosurgeon. He and I always try to help each other. We have great professional respect for each other and have no commercial relationship.

Dr Hegde has connected me to two great doctors, the cardiac surgeon Dr Devi Shetty of Narayana Hrudayalaya and the orthopaedic surgeon Dr Sharan Patil of SPARSH, on various occasions. These are evangelists who have their own connectors and are also invariably connected to other evangelists.

That is how Dr Shetty has connected me to the noted ophthalmologist Dr Bhujang Shetty of Narayana Nethralaya. And of course, I am also connected to the network of connectors and mavens that each of these evangelists has.

So, though I am not a doctor, through my connection with Dr Hegde, I can get high-quality, near-instant attention on any issue from this entire spectrum of the medical community.

Now imagine how the picture would fan out for me in the writing world if I spelt out a similar network of journalists, editors and publishers.

Consider yet another group that comes from the industry to which I belong. Then we can list a group of educators and then government servants, then other professional groups—and very soon we would need a 12 ft x 12 ft wall to depict the entire picture!

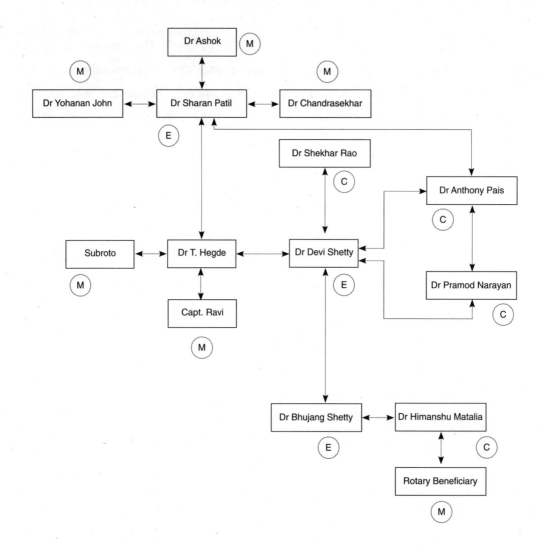

Imagine the power of the network as it occurred in the following real instances:

- I get a call saying that a bus has run over a MindTree employee and she is fighting for her life in a hospital. The doctor there wants to amputate a leg. We need to know if this is drastic; can the leg be saved? We do not know the doctors in this hospital; neither does her family. Instant communication with Dr Sharan Patil establishes that the amputation is indeed needed and we decide to shift her to his hospital. We can trust their professional attention, are assured of empathy and there is no need to speculate on the cost. Because it is a MindTree employee, Dr Ashok, the plastic surgeon, Dr Yohanan John, the anaesthesiologist, and Dr Chandrasekhar, the orthopaedic surgeon, get into top gear. A life is saved and the MindTree employee returns to near normal.

- A visiting customer from overseas collapses due to high blood pressure. My administrator Shanti calls Dr Devi Shetty's office. On arrival at the hospital, he is wheeled straight into emergency and a bevy of doctors examines him. He is kept overnight for observation and, upon becoming better, is released. As a result of this attention, the customer is convinced he and his business are in good hands.

- Dr Pais and Dr Narayan are cancer specialists. They know Dr Sharan Patil and Dr Shetty. I need attention in a particular case and I get instantly connected.

- Dr Himanshu Matalia is an eye surgeon who sees poor patients referred by Rotary International for free. He comes across a particular individual with a high physical disability. He believes an electric wheelchair will make a huge difference to this person. Dr Matalia knows Dr Bhujang Shetty who knows Dr Devi Shetty and thus knows me. I am contacted and through my connections, in turn, the individual gets an electric wheelchair.

- At MindTree, we want our experts to study how professionals in high-pressure jobs do 'scrum reviews'. I request Dr Patil who allows a group of our people to sit in a scrum review by doctors at the start of the day when, behind closed doors, doctors take stock of the events of the previous day and look at what went well and what did not.

- A child who requires major cardiac intervention is brought to Bangalore. The father cannot afford the cost of heart surgery. He works for a friend in faraway Bhubaneswar. I get a call from the friend. Without even sorting out the financial details, Dr Shetty asks the child to be admitted. A number of foundations get involved to provide financial aid. Dr Shetty waives much of the hospital charges and the cardiologist Dr Rao does not charge his professional fees.

In the space below, please draw a similar diagram of mavens, connectors and evangelists for yourself in your own professional field; do take a non-medical example.

Now, list the names of three connectors in your network, including your own.

1.

2.

3.

List the names of three evangelists connected to your connectors.

1.

2.

3.

Now, answer the following questions:

1. When was the last time you created something of value for your connector?

2. Do any two of your evangelists know how good you are at your work? What have you recently done to be on their mind?

3. Do you ever meet or talk to any of these people without an agenda?

4. Do other people's mavens depend on you for anything ever?

19

Future Vision

All of us have the great ability to imagine a future and then go on to create it for ourselves and for others around us. In fact, we are told that in all creation it is only human beings that have a certain perception of what we call the future. All other life forms have an understanding of things past at the most, and live mostly in the present.

When we imagine a future, it has the great power of pulling us towards it as if by an invisible force. The power of vision is at work, every day of our lives. Many of us are in our current profession or calling because someone had a vision of a future when it was not a reality. An uncle said, study commerce and you will make a good auditor. A parent said, you should become a doctor or a lawyer; or maybe you yourself had this one vision to be a journalist and one day you became that.

Look at this workbook as an example. When I wrote the original book, *The Professional*, I had no idea that one day I may create something useful like this that many people may need and hopefully benefit from. But it was a vision in the mind of my publisher Udayan Mitra who lived with the idea until it got imprinted in my mind as well—and lo and behold, it pulled me towards it magically.

> Vision = an image of the future + a plan + serious execution

In the pages that follow, can we picture a future for ourselves and for our loved ones?

A VISION FOR MYSELF

Your vision statement: 'I want to pursue higher education in the following areas in the next five years either as part of a structured learning programme or by tapping into non-formal sources.'

Write down why you want to do this and how you would go about it.

I want to achieve the following material success in the next five to ten years:

I want to achieve the following personal dreams in the next five years, starting next year and continuing each year after that:

I am making the following health and fitness goals for myself, starting with a medical check-up in the next thirty days:

Here is my personal vision for my spouse and this is how I can be of great help:

Here is my vision statement about my child(ren) and this is how I will help them achieve the same:

These are some of my visions for my own self and my family that so far have not fructified and these are the reasons why:

I can still make a difference to myself and my family and here are the trade-offs I must make for achieving my goals:

Goals   **Trade-off necessary**

1.

2.

3.

4.

5.

6.

7.

8.

20

Making an Effective Job Change

One of the most flattering moments in a professional's life comes when the phone rings and at the other end is a head hunter.

Instantly the individual makes you feel very important. Someone has noticed you and wants you for this very critical, very impactful and strategic assignment!

Then, of course, you also like the fact that the job is 'extremely challenging' and can lead to great global assignments after three years. It is a 'multinational company' and the salary is almost double of what you currently get.

The company has had a few false starts in India all right, but with someone like you, it will grow well, the voice says.

What are the questions you would ask yourself after the call? Can you list twenty?

1.

2.

3.

4.

5.

6.

7.

8.

9.

10.

11.

12.

13.

14.

15.

16.

17.

18.

19.

20.

What personal and professional factors would you seriously consider in order to pursue the lead given by the head hunter?

1.

2.

3.

4.

5.

6.

7.

8.

9.

10.

WHAT IS TRULY IMPORTANT FOR ME?

You cannot have everything. Choose how much of what you would happily give up without regrets.

- Big money or your need for independence?
- Sticking to your own competence or trying out a much larger job for which you really have had no training?
- Great career progression or more time with your family?
- A terminally ill parent who requires your presence or a joining bonus large enough to pay for your child's education in the US?

What about your batch mate, who seems to be flourishing after making that great job change a couple of years back? What do you think are the choices they made?

If someone else you know would probably map their needs very differently, you may not want to compare yourself with that individual irrespective of the amount of money they make or the power they yield.

Similarly, when a head hunter tempts you with something that is not important for you, you need not suffer from a false attraction. Writing down what is important to you and what the trade-offs are is a great way to make reasonable career decisions.

While making a professional choice, what weightage would you give to each point in the list of personal and professional factors you drew up above, and up to what point would you make a concession for them? Write a note to yourself in the space below.

Obviously, life is not all that simple. The factors that sometimes kick in are far more that just ten. Try the same exercise now, seeing all the factors at play together.

A possible scenario is as follows.

On the one hand is the new job you have been offered. This is what it involves:

- Organization has flexible views on integrity.
- The pay is fabulous.
- The job requires you to bring in big deals.
- High rate of burnout but top 5 per cent employees are very rich.
- Requires relocation to a great foreign country.
- Child's schooling wouldn't be as good there.
- Parents will need to go to old age home.

On the other hand is your current job. This is what it involves:

- Small, slower company.
- Does not require you to compromise your values.
- Job profile is large.
- Will not be able to pay for son's college fees at a foreign university.
- Sometimes you do think a second house would be nice to have.

The idea is to make a choice where you do not get falsely attracted to things that may not give you sustainable fulfilment.

Please decide now what you would choose to do in the above scenario, given the above pros and cons.

Please write a note below about any conflicting choices you had to resolve in your personal–professional life to arrive at a decision.

Did you ever have to make a choice where you were on the horns of a dilemma?

How did you deal with it?

Have you decided to make a job change? Use this checklist as a set of critical questions to ask yourself.

	Yes	No
1. Have I spent enough time on the company's website to learn about their business?	☐	☐
2. Do I know some of their major customers?	☐	☐
3. Do I know who their suppliers are? Do they treat the suppliers well?		
4. Do I know what ex-employees say about them?	☐	☐
5. Do I know who they compete with and what the competitors say about them?		
6. Are they willing to let me speak to some of their people before I make up my mind?	☐	☐
7. If I google the company, do I know what I will see on message boards?	☐	☐
8. Do I know what my roles and responsibilities will be?	☐	☐
9. Do I really have the knowledge, skills and attitude for these role and responsibilities?	☐	☐
10. Do I know what I would do in the company after three years of being in the job—what has been the typical trajectory for people like me?	☐	☐
11. Have I looked at their financials?	☐	☐
12. If they are privately held, are they forthcoming in discussing key financial details?	☐	☐
13. Do I have a reasonable idea of how I could make a difference to the company hiring me?	☐	☐
14. Will the company give me a thorough induction to get to know them?	☐	☐
15. Are there signs of conflict of interest in the company I should know about?	☐	☐

	Yes	No
16. Do I know the reasons the company has been in the news in the last couple of years?	☐	☐
17. Who do I know that works there? Have I made contact with them?	☐	☐
18. Were there any signs during the hiring process that sent out amygdalic alerts? Should I be taking these more seriously? Am I telling myself that the snake is actually a rope?	☐	☐
19. Did I sit down and thoroughly discuss the job and the prospects with all my immediate family members?	☐	☐
20. Am I getting carried away by the job title?	☐	☐
21. Is this a smaller job than what I have today?	☐	☐
22. Am I thinking of taking this up to prove a point to my current boss?	☐	☐
23. Did I explore an alternative assignment in my current company and tell HR that if I could not have it I might have to consider outside alternatives?	☐	☐
24. In my eagerness to get hired, did I hold off asking an important question to the hirer?	☐	☐
25. Do I know why they let go of the last incumbent?	☐	☐
26. Has he/she become larger in professional stature than before inside or outside the company? Can I speak to him/her?	☐	☐
27. Am I running away from something?	☐	☐
28. Is this job going to be demanding enough or is it a cushy job?	☐	☐
29. If it is a ceremonial job, am I ready for it?	☐	☐
30. Might this job change actually make me professionally obscure after a few years?	☐	☐

And finally, if this list is not relevant for me, am I going to write one that makes sense?

21

Seeing the Big Picture

Most professionals who level out beyond a point in their career usually lack two things:

- the ability to think about the big picture while dealing with immediate problems, and
- critical questioning

Both these abilities are innate but they can be improved by observation, practised and perfected. Each time you consciously practise them and observe things with these two criteria in mind, you get better at them.

The two are interdependent: the more you critically question, the better your ability to see the big picture—and the more you construct the big picture, the more you get to unearth critical questions.

The purpose is simple: going beyond quick fixes and getting to solutions that are sustainable.

Leading professionals seem to have this capacity in abundant measure. What may be examples of big picture thinking?

Imagine a highway congestion problem. During peak traffic, a particular four-lane highway is getting choked. The apparent solution to decongest is obvious: create more capacity. Someone suggests adding an additional lane. But, once built with considerable effort and cost, the commissioned extra lane does not solve the problem. The reason? Now that there is an additional lane, drivers start mindlessly cutting into it; when everyone tries doing that, it creates even more of a traffic jam than before. The authorities here did not anticipate driver psychology. If drivers are not trained in better driving, the additional lane does not serve any purpose.

There is an (in)famous story about Delhi Police who were once called in to fight software piracy by confiscating software duplicated without licence. After a particular raid, the policemen took away sackloads of pirated floppy disks. Then they punctured the floppies with a needle and strung these together to be produced in a court of law as evidence. The uneducated policemen did not realize they were damaging the magnetic media by making holes in them. Before the law enforcers were called to protect intellectual property, someone needed to think of training them on what intellectual property consists of.

Then there is the story from the early 1990s when a trainload of commandos arrived in Bangalore to smoke out the infamous forest brigand Veerappan. He had remained elusive for decades because he operated in the jungles connecting the three southern states of Karnataka, Tamil Nadu and Kerala. There he ruled the roost poaching ivory and perpetrating terror among the people and the police alike. The three state governments asked for central assistance to nab him and that is why the commandos arrived. They were admirably well equipped, armed from head to toe. But they had no idea of the terrain. To be effective, they needed expert guides to find their way in the thick forests of the Western Ghats. The only people who knew the forest were the forest guards, who were a ragtag bunch. When they saw the commandos, they became very unhappy with the vast inequity between themselves and the commandos—all the way from benefits and entitlements to, worst of all, their shoes. The forest guards had for years agitated for proper footwear and the state governments did not issue them the necessary gear. So what did they do? They went on a strike. The commandos arrived but could not get into the jungles and just sat in Bangalore while the brigand had the last laugh!

We work in a world where apparent solutions do not work. Highway congestion? Add a lane. Software piracy? Raid the pirates. Brigand in the forest? Move in the commandos. These show a cause-and-effect relationship between a perceived problem and what sounds like an obvious solution or one most immediately visible.

The truth is that there are usually causes behind causes. Unless we get to the bottom of it all, to the root cause, we cannot build lasting solutions.

Consider the following examples:

Singapore is a small city state where space is at a premium. The state depends on migrant workers from neighbouring Thailand. The workers come in hordes, mostly manual labourers who work on construction sites. Having no family to return to during weekends, they invariably occupied the few open spaces they found next to residential neighbourhoods where they met, made merry, drank and often became unruly, much to the annoyance of the locals who complained to the police. Singapore police did something unusual. Common sense would suggest using force or the threat of it and driving the workers away—but in the process, one would just shift them to another neighbourhood where they would stay until someone else complained. The root cause was not the disturbance the workers were causing, it was their loneliness—having left hearth and home—and the consequent need for community. So Singapore police came up with a counter-intuitive solution. Instead of breaking up the groups, they encouraged them to build weekend communities, arranged for space for congregations and set up food stalls and stages for bands to play on. Instead of finding ad-hoc space and getting hounded out, the migrant workers now congregated in controlled spaces, mingled, made music and were happy.

At MindTree, during the early days, I came across a quaint problem that surfaced when a newly hired employee quit. I was told he was leaving us to go back to his hometown in Kerala. When I spoke to him at length, I found to my surprise that the pressure to leave us came from his mother. He was her only son and she wanted him to work closer to home. To her, the name MindTree meant nothing. It was just another company. So, we decided to start a company newsletter specifically aimed at parents, who could now discern why MindTree would be a career builder and not just another employer for their wards. It was created carefully, attention was paid to the content, and we made sure it had enough stories showing the kind of work our people got to do, how they could grow within the organization and why it was the better choice in the long run. Among other things, we chose a large font size for the magazine to suit the eyes of a fifty-something adult! *The Circle of Life*, as it was called, was an instant hit among parents of MindTree Minds. It was particularly successful because children often did not explain to parents what they did at work, with the common refrain, 'You will not understand.' Now we have a sphere of favourable influence for employee bonding via their parental homes.

A few years ago, I spent a week in a vineyard in the Ahr Valley in Germany, where some of the nicest grapes grow on the mountain slopes. The only person with whom I could have a conversation during my stay was the farmer himself, who grew the grapes and then made wine from them. When I was taking a walk in the vineyard I saw many small birds. These birds ate some of the fruit. I asked the farmer the way out of the destruction and loss that surely troubled him. Interestingly, he said no, it did not. Then he explained to me how, many years ago, they used to spray the crop with pesticides. That drove the little birds away. When the little birds went away, the birds of prey went away too. When the birds of prey went away, the vineyards were overtaken by rodents. The farmer explained to me that nature provides enough for all the parties involved and there is interconnectedness and mutual dependency in every system. It is important for us to view everything as a part of a larger system.

From the examples just discussed, can you think of a problem from your day-to-day living or at work that needs big picture thinking and which you would now look at differently from the way you did in the past? Can you write a note on it for yourself?

Big picture thinking requires continuous questioning. The Japanese are masters at it. They use a famous process called '5 Why and 1 How'. They believe that by asking 'Why' five times, you are highly likely to come to the root cause of a problem and then by exploring 'How', you come to the sustainable solution to the problem.

Consider an employee who has come late to work having the following conversation with a supervisor:

Supervisor:	Why are you late?
Employee:	I missed the bus.
Supervisor:	Why did you miss the bus?
Employee:	I got up late.
Supervisor:	Why did you get up late?
Employee:	I slept late because my wife is unwell.
Supervisor:	Why is your wife not well?
Employee:	We ate at a restaurant over the weekend and the food did not agree with her.

Now, instead of punishing the employee for coming late, the supervisor would do well to ask how he can help. Would the employee like to go home early? Would he like to take the day off, spend some time with his wife, and come back in a better state of mind to take care of work? The supervisor can ask another worker to share the load or simply ask the worker to work from home.

Now, suppose you have the following conversation with yourself.

Me: Why am I overweight?
Answer: I do not exercise.
Me: Why don't I exercise?
Answer: I do not have the time.
Me: Why don't I have the time?
Answer: I sleep late so I get up late and rush to work.
Me: Why do I sleep late and get up late?
Answer: I watch late-night movies.
Me: Why do I watch late-night movies?
Answer: I have stopped reading.

Now, the ultimate question:

How do I restart a good reading habit that takes me away from late-night television watching?

Answer: Buy the kind of books that I once loved reading and get back my reading habit!

A great tool for big picture thinking is the fishbone diagram that helps us to create a big picture while solving problems and draws attention to the interconnected nature of things. More on this in the next page.

KAORU ISHIKAWA AND THE FISHBONE DIAGRAM

Kaoru Ishikawa was a revered Japanese quality expert. He taught the world the idea of looking at any problem through a set of four to six broad paths.

Let us imagine a child who is not doing well at school. There could be many reasons beyond the apparent. These could be classified under four major categories: student, parent, teacher and school related. Ishikawa taught us to put the problem statement of the child not doing well at the head of a fish and start drawing the spine from there. The four major categories then form four sub-spines. In each category, we chart a possible reason. Then we keep asking 'Why' to arrive at a root cause of the problem. Once we come to a root cause, we arrive at a suggested fix by asking 'How'.

Once the entire diagram is finished, we carefully look at which two or three items from the maze of actionable items, if worked upon, would have the most impact. Remember the 80:20 rule–80 per cent of all impact can come by choosing the right 20 per cent of the actionable items. The idea is not to do too many things, nor to dissipate energy, but to focus on the right set of a few things.

Look at the fishbone diagram on the facing page that illustrates the problem of the child not doing well at school by identifying the principal factors that might be causing the problem, and analysing the possible reasons under each factor.

The Japanese use the fishbone diagram as a great problem-solving tool. It can be used very well in groups. A group decides what could be the four to six major factors involved—in the case of the previous example, these are the student, parents, teacher and school. The group can identify these drivers by having a round table conversation. Then the group takes up each factor and brainstorms on possible reasons and the root cause for each such reason, to finally nail down what, if fixed, can be the solution. At the end, when you look at the fishbone in its entirety, there appear to be many solutions. The group votes to choose the top three solutions it would focus on and implements these. The effect is monitored over time and modified as may be needed.

Fishbone Analysis of Parent-Student-School-Teacher

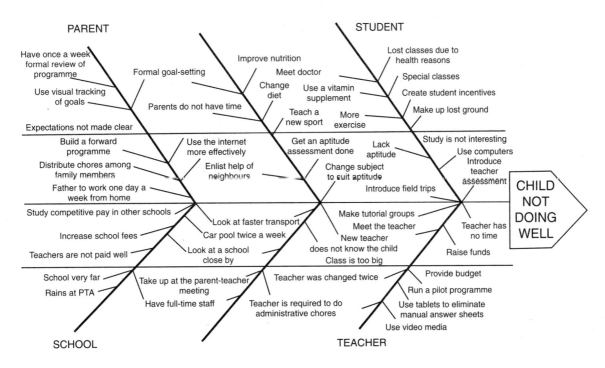

Now let us consider a work-related problem: let us imagine that we have defective parts produced from an assembly line causing losses through rework, loss of production time and customer satisfaction. Now, let us put that as a problem statement ('Defective Parts' in this case), make that problem the fish head, draw a spine and then create four sub-spines as Men, Material, Money and Information. Can you simulate a fishbone exercise by yourself based on these four parameters? Use the facing page.

DEFECTIVE PARTS FISHBONE DIAGRAM

22

Critical
Questioning

The difference between a great professional in any field and an average one is often the ability to ask critical questions.

The word 'critical' here means 'crucial'. Critical questioning is a function of critical thinking. Both critical thinking and questioning can be cultivated over time and refined. To appreciate the concept, please read the following passage very carefully:

On the night of 25 July 2012, Arjun Trivedi received a call at home after midnight. He was the head of administration at MindTree, a software development company based in Bangalore that maintained a 24x7 facility to serve its worldwide customers in developing and maintaining solutions for mission critical applications. The call came from the security supervisor of Building 1 at their Mysore Road facility in Bangalore. The facility had a rivulet running through it in a south–north direction and it joined an erstwhile river that had turned into a sewage discharge drain that flowed past the campus in an east–west direction. There was unusually heavy rain that night that had caught everyone off-guard. Water overflow had taken place and it went right into the basement of the five-floor Phase 1 building; 40,000 sq. ft of software development space was damaged along with the network cable that went underground. Power shut down. There was a large capacity generator set that got flooded from below all the way up to about two feet from the ground. Arjun took a quick debrief on the phone, got out of bed, changed rapidly and jumped into his car. On the way, he phoned his deputy and asked him to come immediately to the building as also to call in all hands on deck.

When he reached the place, it turned out to be a nightmarish experience. Several questions ran through his head as he surveyed the devastation. By this time his deputy Vivian and his assistant Ismail had landed up. Arjun asked all of them to get into a first floor conference room and go to a whiteboard to draw out an action plan and distribute responsibilities for damage control.

From the situation you just read about, without going back to the previous page, please do the following:

Describe the event in four sentences:

Name the actors and tell us their roles in the sequence of their appearance:

Identify the cause of the incident:

Note the amount of damage caused to the facility:

Observe if the incidence and/or the damage were avoidable:

The interesting thing about the exercise you just did was that the answers were all there in the passage you previously read. So, what you did in reality was to *describe, name, identify, note, define, observe* and *recite*.

This is how we routinely process information as we deal with day-to-day incidents. This is called **literal thinking** and this process, while important, does not yield any near-term actionable options.

For that, you would need to:

- Analyse

- Synthesize

- Compare and Contrast

- Infer

- Sequence

Please ask a set of questions on behalf of Arjun that would help in each of the categories above and write them down in the space below each item.

Now go ahead and simulate the whiteboard exercise to draw a damage control plan for the team.

The exercise so far has been a powerful way to deploy resources to contain immediate damage and create a recovery path that would bring operations back on its feet.

But is that all there is to it?

If you were Arjun, what would you have done?

Please jot down your thoughts and ideas in the space below:

As a great professional, your job is to 'think beyond factual knowledge'. Arjun and his team should be good enough by themselves to recover from the setback with all the 'literal' data points on hand. Your task is to think beyond these. So, here is what you need to do: think of each of the words below and step up the critical questioning based on the big picture.

- Evaluate

- Imagine

- Predict

- Speculate

- Judge

- Hypothesize

23

Being Prepared

Answer the following questions truthfully:

	Yes	No
1. I usually look before I leap.	☐	☐
2. I have rarely forgotten a task on hand.	☐	☐
3. I seek a good reason why I should attend a meeting.	☐	☐
4. I research people from their website, LinkedIn, Google and Wikipedia before I meet up with them.	☐	☐
5. I read the circulated papers before attending a meeting and make mental notes.	☐	☐
6. I have a to-do list at any time.	☐	☐
7. Before packing up for the day, I look at the calendar for tomorrow.	☐	☐
8. All my presentations from the last few years are on a backed-up external hard disk.	☐	☐
9. I anticipate the questions customers may ask and simulate the conversation in my mind before a meeting.	☐	☐
10. I invariably find the customer meeting goes the way I had simulated it in my mind.	☐	☐
11. When I am in charge of an event, I start with a control chart.	☐	☐
12. Before my team goes to negotiate, I do a mock negotiation with them.	☐	☐
13. I ask a colleague to play devil's advocate before an important decision.	☐	☐
14. When all is going well, I look at what may go wrong.	☐	☐
15. I know the emergency exits in my office.	☐	☐

	Yes	No
16. I am almost always on time for any meeting.	☐	☐
17. If I am likely to be late, I send out an SMS to attendees.	☐	☐
18. I fill up gas in the car before the needle hits the quarter tank mark.	☐	☐
19. I know where my bank papers, house mortgage documents and previous years' income tax returns are.	☐	☐
20. I backed up my computer at least once in the last thirty days.	☐	☐
21. I do not keep things until the last minute.	☐	☐
22. I complete things that do not please me but must get done.	☐	☐
23. Sometimes I spend more time planning than executing.	☐	☐
24. I know where the fuse box is located in my house.	☐	☐
25. I know where the tool kit and the spare wheel is in my car.	☐	☐
26. I have an umbrella.	☐	☐
27. I keep a jacket and tie in the office.	☐	☐
28. At the end of a meeting, I jot down action points emanating from it for myself.	☐	☐
29. I periodically call teammates and do a structured debrief even if there is nothing significant to report.	☐	☐
30. I do not believe no news is good news.	☐	☐

The brain is a storage device and it is primarily used for storing memories. It is interesting that memories are always about things past. But then, there are some people who can actually create memories for the future!

More and more, as leaders among professionals, we must deal with what are called 'unscripted events'. In other words, these are not things you may have been trained for. You may not have precedence of any kind to deal with such unfolding events.

Psychologists tell us that when faced with an altogether new situation and given many options, the brain sides with what may seem familiar to it. So, the one who thinks ahead, thinks of alternative possibilities, thinks of decisional options and their respective consequences is the one who is building memories of the future.

This is the one who is less likely to be in a traffic jam, miss a flight, fumble for answers or have to say 'sorry'.

24

Negotiating New World Imperatives

Answer the following ten questions truthfully:

	Yes	No
1. I look at a co-worker as a fellow professional and not primarily as a man or a woman.	☐	☐
2. I would feel proud to work for a manager who happens to be a woman.	☐	☐
3. When staffing a project, I do not presuppose a woman colleague cannot take a role that requires long hours and physical discomforts.	☐	☐
4. At an official dinner, I make sure women colleagues do not feel left out because of the invisible male-ring.	☐	☐
5. I do not think the term 'customer' necessarily means a man.	☐	☐
6. I understand the meaning of sexual harassment.	☐	☐
7. While speaking to a visiting delegation, I am conscious not to focus only on one or two senior people.	☐	☐
8. I do not make gender-insensitive statements.	☐	☐
9. I do not forward jokes disparaging women and minorities.	☐	☐
10. I know how sexual harassment allegations need to be addressed in my organization.	☐	☐

One of the signs of a developed economy is the percentage of women in white-collar jobs. That number in western countries matches the number of men at work—quite a feat given that before the 1950s, even in America, not many women went to work in offices.

It is a relatively new phenomenon in India and most sectors right now have less than 20 per cent of its workforce as women.

As more women join in, professional men must be sensitized to gender issues and not just get educated on issues related to sexual harassment at work. Good professionals, whether employed by an organization or running their own set-up, must proactively seek training in matters related to gender issues.

Answer the following ten questions:

	Yes	No
1. I understand the meaning of the following terms:		
a. Global warming	☐	☐
b. Greenhouse gases	☐	☐
c. Carbon footprint	☐	☐
d. Emission	☐	☐
e. Recycling	☐	☐
f. Energy-efficient	☐	☐
g. Landfill	☐	☐
h. Biodegradable	☐	☐
2. I know how my profession can adversely impact sustainability.	☐	☐
3. I know how my profession can positively impact sustainability.	☐	☐
4. I switch off electricity consuming devices when not in use.	☐	☐
5. I segregate wet and dry garbage at home.	☐	☐
6. I know how to properly dispose of old batteries and electronics junk.	☐	☐
7. I know how my eating habits impact the planet.	☐	☐
8. I know that my business has stakeholders beyond shareholders, customers and employees.	☐	☐
9. I do not use plastic, styrofoam and other non-biodegradable material.	☐	☐
10. I know where our office garbage goes at the end of the day.	☐	☐

The issue is not whether the polar ice cap is melting and several species are going to vanish forever.

Today, every profession, bar none, has a definitive carbon footprint as well as the capacity to prevent it.

As a doctor running my own clinic, am I careful about medical waste? As an office manager in a bank, do I bring in paper cups, better still reusable mugs, for use, rather than use plastic cups that choke the drain or are burnt by garbage disposal agencies and contribute to lung diseases with their toxic emission?

Large organizations guzzle water to maintain lawns, and use outdated electrical appliances that are not energy-efficient. What about rainwater harvesting, garbage segregation and use of solar power that every one of us can take up?

Then, of course, there are other sustainability issues like work practices with our sub-contractors that we need to understand. It is not about compliance; sustainability-sensitive professionals will automatically be seen as responsible and be sought out by global customers who are increasingly asking for it.

Answer the following ten questions:

	Yes	No
1. I know and respect the laws that govern my profession.	☐	☐
2. I know and respect the laws that govern my organization.	☐	☐
3. In matters of law, I do not assume things. I reach for an expert.	☐	☐
4. I know the liability my work can cause.	☐	☐
5. I know that I and my organization may be legally liable wherever we may do business in the world and not just in the home country.	☐	☐
6. I know the meaning of the term 'insider trading'.	☐	☐
7. I understand the gift policy of my organization.	☐	☐
8. I know what legal returns must be submitted by my company from time to time.	☐	☐
9. I know the implication of bribery and money laundering under the law.	☐	☐
10. I understand the meaning of the term 'disclosure'. I disclose when in doubt.	☐	☐

Many celebrated professionals of global repute have fallen from their pinnacle because they forgot the simple principles behind one or more of the ten questions you just answered. When they fell, it was with the loud crash of a porcelain doll on a marble floor. Their reputation was in tatters and could never be put back together again.

Governance is not just about my own sense of right and wrong but it is all about demonstrable action.

Tick what you know from the following ten questions:

1. I understand that calling a person of African origin a 'negro' or 'black' is offensive, as is calling a person of Asian origin a 'chinky'. We cannot make a reference to someone through that person's colour, race, religion and sexual orientation.
2. I cannot make disparaging comments or discriminate against anyone, particularly against minorities and gays or lesbians.
3. It is not appropriate to ask personal questions to someone without permission from the individual.
4. Two adults living together or having children does not mean they have to be married and the subject merits no conversation in a professional relationship.
5. Table manners require me not to pile up food on my plate, lick my fingers, burp or ignore others who may be eating with us.
6. I seek clarifications on cultural appropriateness before engaging with someone from another country, particularly in a business setting.
7. All white people are not Americans, and vice versa.
8. I say 'please' and 'thank you' when speaking to others. I send handwritten 'thank you' notes to a host after being invited to a lunch or dinner.
9. I do not depend on non-verbal communication like nodding my head to convey a yes or a no. I say yes or no and frequently check the other person's comprehension.
10. I speak up every time I do not understand something. I do not remain silent when I am confused.

Cross-cultural understanding is crucial for every professional. The ten questions above barely scratch the surface of the subject.

A cross-culturally savvy professional is a great global asset in today's world. Most people learn about cross-cultural issues by trial and error. It does not have to be that way.

Many self-employed professionals like doctors, lawyers and real-estate agents in India are dealing extensively with people of non-Indian origin but do not understand the nuances. It is always a good idea to get formally trained or at least read up literature on the subject.

Cross-cultural skills create an atmosphere of trust in a relationship and lead to great business and personal success.

Check your knowledge of the following:

1. I know the meaning of the following terms:
   a. Copyright
   b. Patents
   c. Trademarks
2. My organization's business plan, structure, customer list and employee list are confidential.
3. I may not discuss my compensation and benefits with anyone other than HR and my manager.
4. I do not leave meeting papers behind me in the conference room.
5. I shred classified documents I no longer need.
6. When leaving my company for another, I cannot take along what is on the hard disk of my official computer; my Rolodex would be the property of my organization.
7. I cannot discuss official projects I am involved in with friends and family.
8. I know the liability of downloading content on my official computer and these need not be restricted to software code.
9. I know what the term 'open source' means and what the implication may be for using material available for free under such a source to create something that may be different but is derived from it.
10. I clean the whiteboard in the conference room each time after I use it.

There was a time when the most important possession for someone was land, a house and cattle.

Ownership of material objects such as these were protected by law. Everyone was expected not to trespass on what may belong to someone else and basic understanding of what constituted mine and thine was well understood.

During the last century, more than material property, intellectual property like copyright, trademarks and patents have become valuable. The patented formula behind Coke is more valuable than all the Coke bottling plants put together. The trademarks as in the Niké swoosh-sign and the Apple logo are more valuable than the individual products that carry them.

Even as my books or your music may be accessible on the Internet, someone cannot simply start unauthorized use of these because they come under copyright protection.

The idea of intellectual property (IP) is relatively new and there is little formal education among professionals on this. As a result, many people routinely violate IP regulations and contractual obligations due to their ignorance.

25

A Leader among Professionals

Answer the following questions:

	Yes	No
1. I frequently visit my organization's website to check updates.	☐	☐
2. I have an updated slide deck on my organization.	☐	☐
3. I have a slide deck on my own function based on the mission, vision and values of my organization.	☐	☐
4. I use the slide deck to bring colleagues on board.	☐	☐
5. I use the slide deck before signing up a new business partner or a supplier.	☐	☐
6. I know my own roles and responsibilities clearly and discuss these with my boss once in six months to keep them relevant.	☐	☐
7. I seek feedback proactively for my function.	☐	☐
8. I provide feedback proactively.	☐	☐
9. I read the customer satisfaction survey in detail.	☐	☐
10. I read the employee satisfaction survey in detail.	☐	☐
11. I voice disagreement if the organization's interests are being put at stake.	☐	☐
12. I have been trained to handle the press.	☐	☐
13. I spoke about my organization and our work in at least one external forum in the last six months.	☐	☐
14. A significant customer win in the last six months was attributed to me.	☐	☐
15. I am not at a loose end when it comes to looking at the week ahead.	☐	☐
16. I track where my time goes.	☐	☐

	Yes	No
17. Colleagues reach out to me on organizational matters and solicit advice.	☐	☐
18. I know the functioning of various parts of the organization quite well.	☐	☐
19. I fully disclose any conflict of interest before it happens.	☐	☐
20. I am asked to join interview panels for senior hires outside my function.	☐	☐
21. I understand the financial aspects of my organization well.	☐	☐
22. I know the budgeting process and all major costs of the organization.	☐	☐
23. I always find my successor.	☐	☐
24. I mentor people outside my function.	☐	☐
25. I have a point of view on the ecosystem in which my organization functions.	☐	☐
26. I feel I have a lot more to contribute to my profession.	☐	☐
27. I confront value breaches irrespective of the discomfort to me and others.	☐	☐
28. I am taking care of my health.	☐	☐
29. Even though I sometimes feel unhappy with my work and organization, I am proud of both.	☐	☐
30. I know where the growth opportunities for the organization are and I am actively pursuing these.	☐	☐
31. Many opinion leaders outside the organization know me quite well.	☐	☐
32. I periodically teach at a leading educational institution.	☐	☐
33. I fired a few incompetent people in the last three years.	☐	☐

	Yes	No
34. Regulators ask for my opinion before making policy changes.	☐	☐
35. The press asks me for my opinion in matters of importance in my area of work.	☐	☐
36. People often request me to share my slides.	☐	☐
37. I have been published in a leading journal in the last one year.	☐	☐
38. Fellow professionals read what I blog.	☐	☐
39. I serve on cross-functional committees outside my function.	☐	☐
40. Half of the top ten customers of my organization know me.	☐	☐
41. I influenced a major policy change in my organization in the last couple of years.	☐	☐
42. I have reduced cost and it has been noticed how I was able to do it.	☐	☐
43. I spend white-space time with peers and subordinates.	☐	☐
44. I listen well.	☐	☐
45. I learn from unusual sources and bring my knowledge to my organization.	☐	☐
46. The board members know me.	☐	☐
47. I represent my organization in industry associations and forums.	☐	☐
48. I brace unpopularity to get things done.	☐	☐
49. I have made three significant mistakes in the last five years.	☐	☐
50. I do not live off my organization's brand; I contribute to it.	☐	☐

Chances are that only 10 per cent of professionals who have come this far will be able to relate to the fifty questions that were just asked.

Of these, probably only 10 per cent would be able to affirmatively answer many of the questions above.

What, then, was the purpose, you ask?

Is the ultimate test in this workbook designed to make 99 per cent professionals feel inadequate about themselves?

No—that is not the intent.

First of all, these questions are meant for those who have nearly arrived at the peak of their professional standing and feel there is more left to do.

Second, the questions are designed to present areas where there may still be room for improvement.

These fifty questions, answered confidently, present an image of what we may say is a professional's professional. This is what it takes to be admired by peers as a professional par excellence. Practised over time, the attributes, actions and values behind these questions make someone outstanding in any given profession.

These constitute peak performing talent based on my personal observation of hundreds of high-performance individuals who see their profession not just as a source of income but as a platform that holds the purpose of their lives.

We have now come to the end of this workbook.

Use the next couple of pages to write notes to yourself.

Reflect on what you may have learnt, what are the lessons that you would like to implement in your work life, what you would like to do more or less of—finishing with a pen portrait of the kind of professional you want to be.

NOTES

NOTES

PROFESSIONAL RESOURCES

Books

On leadership
Five Minds for the Future by Howard Gardner
Leading with Questions by Michael Marquardt
A Whole New Mind by Daniel Pink
Emotional Intelligence by Daniel Goleman

On self-improvement
It's Not about the Bike by Lance Armstrong
Man's Search for Meaning by Victor Frankel

Videos

On building a personal vision
The Power of Vision by Joel Barker
Infinite Vision: Story of Aravind Eye Hospital
Burden of Dreams by Les Banks

Websites

Professional web resources
www.google.com
www.youtube.com
www.wikipedia.org
www.wikihow.org
www.stanford.edu
http://knowledge.wharton.upenn.edu/

Health (including, very importantly, mental health)
www.nih.gov

ABOUT THE AUTHOR

Subroto Bagchi is co-founder and chairman of MindTree, one of India's most admired software companies.

In 1999, he started as the chief operating officer of MindTree. Soon after, the company was hit by a global economic slowdown and then the events of 9/11. Many start-up companies collapsed during this time, and Bagchi moved to the US as a consequence and helped the leadership team stay together through the difficult years. During this time, he articulated a new positioning for MindTree as the best mid-sized company from India, which later became a reality.

Between 1999 and 2007, he was instrumental in articulating MindTree's mission, vision and values. He led leadership development, marketing and knowledge management initiatives that differentiated the company from the very beginning. MindTree's distinctive physical locations reflect his thought leadership. He is also the face of the company's outreach beyond business. In 2007, he was part of the apex team that led MindTree from an idea to IPO.

Post-IPO, Bagchi took on the role of Gardener at MindTree. In this new role, he focused full-time on the top 100 leaders at MindTree so as to expand their leadership capacity beyond the founding team. In 2010, he was appointed vice chairman to the board. On 1 April 2012, he assumed the office of chairman.

Bagchi is on the board of governors of the Indian Institute of Management, Bangalore, and a member of the governing council of the Software Technology Parks of India. He is a well-known writer, having penned a number of widely read books and columns for newspapers and magazines. In 2011, he was acclaimed as India's no.1 bestselling business author.